MIND IN SPO...

# MIND IN SPORT
## Directing Energy Flow into Success

KENNETH E JENNINGS

1993
JUTA & CO, LTD

Printed and bound in South Africa by
The Rustica Press, Ndabeni, Cape.

The author and publisher wish to thank *The Sunday Times* and *Beeld* for permission
to reproduce photographs and Dr Don Beck of the National Values Center, Denton,
USA for kind permission to reproduce 'The Human Spiral', Figure 20.

Cover concept and design: Dellené Jennings and Joy Wrench

D1951

# *Dedication*

To the playful and intuitive child in each one of us
– enjoy the moment!

# Contents

# Acknowledgements

There are always some very special people who make the process of writing a book just a little bit easier.

I found my informal dialogue with John Hunt regarding writing style invaluable. He offered his wisdom and encouragement in the early stages of this manuscript, and provided a clear focus for me to expand my ideas. Our relationship triggered a creative flow of ideas that I found exciting and challenging.

Edward Griffiths, the sports editor of the *Sunday Times*, and Harry Lombaard, the assistant sports editor of the *Beeld*, allowed me free access to their photographic libraries. I am appreciative of their unconditional help while I was under extreme pressure to find meaningful photographic material for the book.

Jimmy Cook, Bruce Fordyce, Brian Mitchell and Jonty Rhodes met with me to share their experiences of mental preparation. Their ideas reinforced my theoretical model regarding MIND IN SPORT. I thank them for giving me the opportunity to clarify my own thinking while listening to their unique experiences during training and actual competition.

I have been most fortunate to have worked with a number of elite sportsmen and sportswomen. This book would not have been possible without their involvement. Unknowingly, they are co-authors of this book.

In meeting with potential publishers, I was fortunate to meet André Struwig of Juta. He immediately sensed the urgency I felt to get this book onto the shelves. I know that the printing and distribution of this book occurred in record time. To Desirée Walker, Pauline de Villiers and Juta, I thank you for moving with the flow of this book to its completion.

I have a very special family team who I love dearly. The concepts of 'shared responsibility', 'being in the boat together' and 'reflective thinking' are very real in our team. My wife Dellené provided the emotional support when the going got tough. Throughout the writing of this book she always put my needs first. She shared my every concern and listened to all my doubts. She was my sounding board. She unselfishly created the necessary space and time for me to write. My two boys, Wayne and Gareth, knew that Dad was hard at work. They sensed the importance of the journey their Dad had embarked on. Never did they disrupt the process. As time went on, they intuitively knew when to move in and connect with me and when to 'disappear' so that I could focus again. In a sense, they journeyed with me in a very natural and easy way.

Finally, I have become more aware of my own thinking patterns while writing. These patterns were first established in my original family where my parents gave encouragement to my own develop- ment as an individual. My ecosystemic training as a psychologist at the University of South Africa provided me with a more sophis- ticated way of looking at and understanding people in interaction. Subsequently, further reading and conferences have influenced the way I think. I can now only think in circles, spirals and waves. I have become sensitive to the delicate balance that exists; we are all connected in the fabric. I am deeply indebted to all those who have in some way shaped my thinking.

Ken Jennings
November 1992

# List of figures

# Introduction

I have had the privilege to consult with top sportsmen, sports-women and teams in a highly competitive South African sporting context. The underlying reason for our meetings was to develop a suitable mental training programme, in order to enhance their performance on the field of play. During my involvement with them, I became aware of the complexity of the phenomenon of mental preparation. The dialogue between us went beyond winning and success motivation.

The dialogue focused on confronting the way the mind operates in action. In discussion, I found that my own thinking was constantly changing. New issues were emerging. New and creative thinking about performance was being triggered in our relationship. Learning was taking place on both sides, as we maintained focus on the journey leading up to competition, as well as the unfolding journey that the athlete has to undertake on the field during actual competition. In all of this, I had to maintain my own focus on preparing teams and individuals to be mentally ready for the demands of tough competition. The quality of the performances on the field often surprised both me and the athlete/team. The end result always seemed to take care of itself.

Competitive Western sport does not condone those who lose. Advertising, sponsorships, media and public involvement have made top elite sport a ruthless, dehumanising experience for our sportsmen. The stresses to contend with are immense. There is little or no room for human error during performance. After the loss to Sri Lanka in the 1992 cricket World Cup in Australia, the South African captain Kepler Wessels stated that he found 'the fickleness and the unrealistic expectations of the South African public to be of deep concern'.

I personally do not think that this is solely a South African phenomenon. British football clubs, for example, have large supporter followings that are not sympathetic to poor performance. Club managers are under tremendous pressure to ensure that their teams are successful. Supporters become emotionally connected to a team and their results. Through the process of identification, supporters are able to derive emotional benefits of wellbeing from the results obtained by their team. Feelings of ecstasy and 'highness' manifest themselves after winning. Depression and 'downness' surface after a loss.

Having stated this, I do believe that sport is the one unifying element in a rapidly changing South Africa. There is a need for the evolution of national pride in the new South Africa, a unity of purpose. One only needs to reflect on how our cricketers were welcomed home after reaching the semi-finals of the World Cup to understand what I mean. The cricket tour of the West Indies provided common ground for conversation in strange company at dinner parties. Watching the Barbados test match on television brought home a realisation that new relationships with past antagonists were not only possible, but were actually a reality.

Participation in the Barcelona Olympics (after 32 years of isolation) has opened up new global connections with nations in a way that was previously thought to be impossible. This offers hope. It also provides meaningful examples of how a connected, integrated globe operates. The playground is sport. Through a process of transference, individuals and communities in the new South Africa can also challenge their 'old' perceptions of past antagonists. New relationships need to be forged between diverse communities in order for our evolving society to provide the healthy synergy of a committed rugby or football team. The playground becomes life.

After my involvement with the Natal rugby team in their historic 18–12 Currie Cup victory against Northern Transvaal at Loftus Versfeld in 1990, I found myself reflecting on the phenomenon of mental training. It is the objective of this book to share with you my own epistemology of healthy mental training. I have named my book *Mind in Sport : Directing Energy Flow into Success* to reflect how I perceive 'mind' to operate in a sporting context. Of significance is how the mind of the athlete and the mind of the coach interact in the build up to competition, as well as how the mind operates during actual performance. In addition, I have tried to examine how individual minds interact to form a team 'mind'.

The intention is to explore:

- **The coming together of Western and Eastern thinking.** Stated differently: is it possible to introduce Eastern philosophy into highly competitive Western sport that is embedded in Western culture?

- **The psychology of winning** that incorporates the basic building blocks for a psychology of being. I believe that the definition of winning needs to be broadened. Success motivation needs to be balanced with the intuitive inner feelings of the athlete. There is no magic formula or 10-step programme to winning. I contend that the psychology of being provides exciting insights and inner challenges to those athletes who transcend the limited definition of winning as being an end result.

- **The phenomenon of quantum leaps in performance**. I will endeavour to sketch for you how team synergy is created. Sporting action is dependent on synchronised energy flow. The mind becomes the activator of directed energy flow. Further, I will examine the nature of upward and downward cycles of performance over time.

- **The psychology of coaching** will be explored through the eyes of the new paradigm (way of thinking). Society finds itself in a crisis as a result of trying to apply concepts of an outdated world view. A new vision of reality, with a fundamental change in our thoughts, perceptions, expectations and values is needed (Capra, 1982). I believe that this new paradigm provides exciting insights into the complexity of sporting performance. In particular, the psychology of coaching needs to relook at how athletes learn. Coaches need to evaluate their own epistemology.

- **The nature of new techniques** which I have developed to enhance performance. Sport is played in space and time, in the nonverbal domain. Therefore it is important to examine the differences in left- and right-brain functioning. The use of music to transcend psychological obstacles will be examined— and how music can become both a relaxer and arouser for competition. In addition, imagery can be used to deal with sporting difficulties and in the process to gain better understanding of self, group, and the relationships in the group. These methods are predominantly right-brain nonverbal experiences that connect in a meaningful way to the nonverbal demands of the playing fields.

• **Going beyond sport** in a new emerging South Africa. This requires us to confront the destruction of violence and understand the dynamic balance of existing connections between opposing forces. In addition, businesses will need to evaluate their thinking as the market decreases and competition increases.

Chapter 1 looks at mind in action. In particular, the focus is on how the mind is thinking and operating while the body is active. In this chapter fundamental elements of Zen philosophy are explored.

The psychology of being is explored in Chapter 2, entitled 'The Psychology of Winning'. I contend that when a person stops seeking techniques to win or achieve, this allows for an inner freedom to perform; creativity and spontaneity surface. I outline those actions or elements which I believe provide the athlete with the opportunity to reach a level of being where mind and body integrate harmoniously.

Chapter 3 focuses on energy flow and quantum leaps in performance. Natural cycles of upward and downward flow during interaction are examined. The philosophy of Taoism is introduced briefly.

In Chapter 4, the psychology of coaching is outlined using the the principles of systems thinking. The concepts of shared responsibility, and awareness and process coaching are covered in detail. Coaching in a South African context, where there is a diversity of values, is explored, using a model of value thinking systems.

Chapter 5 looks at the phenomenon of mental preparation. Elite athletes are always performing under stress. Being able to cope with such demands in a relaxed way is important. In this chapter, I also explore the concept of mental toughness. Further, I look at how music can be used to enhance the standard of performance. I then suggest how to develop your own mental preparation programme.

Chapter 6 goes beyond sport. More specifically, I focus on three topics in this chapter which I believe are of immense importance. Firstly, I examine the potential destructiveness of the use of drugs in sport. Secondly, I explore the changing South Africa and the eruption of violence. Finally, I briefly connect 'mind in business' with some of my fundamental concepts of Mind in Sport.

The ideas I intend sharing with you will provide a different perspective of sports motivation. Motivation is often thought of as being the power of positive thinking and the desire to win at all costs. The question of how to become inwardly motivated is at the core of this book. The power of positive thinking is extended to the idea of 'balance' in thinking. Ideas of 'hyping up' and 'psyching up' are challenged by concepts such as upward and downward energy flow. In a sense, the intention of this book is to challenge your old thinking about motivation.

Motivation is a term that both athletes and coaches hide behind. If a team wins, then the coach and players contend that they were motivated. If a team loses, then the coach and players blame the lack of motivation as the cause of the defeat. The ideas in this book will move beyond the traditional link between winning and motivation. I believe that the phenomenon of motivation is not fully understood. Therefore I will be looking at motivation through different 'spectacles'. Without using the word 'motivation', all my ideas are interconnected to form the key elements of an inwardly balanced and motivated athlete.

Sport can be classified into three main groups:
1. **Interactive team sports**, like rugby, football, field and ice hockey and water polo involve individuals interacting in a team. Both the individual and team need to be looked after. Further, how the individual and the team interact also needs attention. Highly interactive team sports are explosive and physically demanding.
2. **Individual sports (time/distance focus)**, like field and track athletics, marathon running and swimming involve competition against oneself and against opponents in events. The main

focus is the race against time, or the challenge of extending distance in the performance (as in long or high jump, javelin or discus throwing).

3. **Individual sports (process or flow focus)**, like cricket, tennis, karate, boxing, fencing, squash and wrestling involve interaction between self and opponent. Each move you may make is countered by a move from the opponent, which in turn may shape your next move.

I have not geared this book to any one particular sport. While the demands of each sport are uniquely different, I have attempted to look at common themes that may occur in mind during any performance. I have drawn examples from a wide range of sports to highlight certain points. Whilst reading, do not fall into the trap of wanting actual specifics for your particular sport. You will not find them in this book. I have attempted to keep my discussion fairly unstructured, so that the reader can fill in the holes for him/herself.

Meaningful connections between some of the concepts and the demands of your sport need to be made in your unique way. This will ensure meaningful learning. This book does not offer the reader any techniques and 'quick fixes' on how to win and become highly motivated. Instead, it attempts to bring together a series of ideas and thoughts that you yourself will need to integrate into a meaningful whole. The ideas are all interconnected. There is no single logical conclusion.

In order to sketch further practical insights regarding sporting performance, I arranged interviews with some of South Africa's top sportsmen. The intention was to gain some understanding of their philosophy of mental preparation. In particular, I was interested in mapping out elements in their thinking that lead to successful performance. I am priviledged to be able to share their ideas with you. I am indebted to Jonty Rhodes, Jimmy Cook, Bruce Fordyce and Brian Mitchell for giving me the opportunity to meet with them. I had previously developed a relationship with Jonty and Jimmy before writing this book, which made it easy for me to arrange an interview. Nevertheless, I thank them sincerely for giving me the time to ask them some questions that required them to open up to me. In particular, I wish to thank Brian and Bruce who were prepared to meet with me to share some of their personal views about themselves and their outstanding successes in the fields of boxing and ultra marathon running, respectively. All these sportsmen displayed a fundamental trust in our dialogue. I value this, and thank them for giving me further insights into my own thinking.

I have used the term 'sportsman'/'sportswoman'/'athlete' to denote any individual who performs in a sporting context. For the sake of ease of writing I will use the masculine application of sportsman when referring to an individual performer, irrespective of sex. I apologise to those who may feel offended by this sexist style of writing. The main intention is to bypass the sportsman/ sportswoman distinction, as well as to avoid the cumbersome nature of continually stating that I am making references to both sexes. Therefore, throughout this book, take it as an unstated fact that I am always referring to both male and female performer in any particular sporting context, when I use the terms 'sportsman' or 'athlete'.

In some discussions, I may make reference to the concept 'team'. While the ideas being examined may apply to the team, they will also, by virtue of connection, apply to the individual. Coaches of individual athletes should also be able to apply some of the concepts that I may have examined in team sports to their own individual coaching styles. Therefore, any coach could interchange the terms individual and team, so that the concepts can be applied meaningfully to a particular sport.

The book is mainly aimed at the athlete, coach or sports psychologist. Although it is fundamentally aimed at these main interacting 'players' involved in elite sport, I am hoping that any sports lover will find some meaning in my ideas. Although some minds may draw a distinction between sport and life, I am unable to do so. Distinctions are made only by mind. How mind operates in sport is actually no different to how mind operates in any other life situation. Therefore, the book should appeal to anyone who may be interested in examining 'mind in action' operating in any interpersonal context.

Businessmen could apply some of these ideas to working groups. 'Mind in Sport' can become 'Mind in Business'. Business organisations are no different from sporting teams. Employees working in a certain department should have a common purpose in interaction. Departmental synergy is necessary to achieve set targets. Performance and motivation in business are vital in order for profits to be made. Managers have similar problems in motivating employees as do coaches in trying to motivate players. I believe that the assumptions that mind makes during performance need to be carefully examined. Whether it is a business context or sporting context, mind is the pre-determiner of purposeful and directed action.

The ideas shared in this book constantly try and connect deeper philosophical issues with practical sporting issues. However, the ideas can be applied to any interpersonal context. I believe that healthy interpersonal living has at its core an understanding of dynamic balance between interacting forces. The section on stress and relaxation should interest those who feel that they need to reintroduce a balance in their lives. Executives, for example, need to examine their lifestyles. Stress management is a necessary part of healthy living.

For those who are grappling with the issue of self-actualisation, I offer a chapter on the psychology of winning. Do not be fooled by this title, since I was forced to use the term 'winning' because the book had sport as its focus. The chapter is actually concerned with the psychology of being. I outline what I believe constitutes the interpersonal and interactional elements of fully functioning living.

Throughout the book, you will come across terms such as 'dynamic balance', 'connections', 'flow', 'interdependent', 'pattern', 'rhythm', 'relationships', 'participation', 'process', 'evolution', 'quantum leaps', 'synergy', 'wave-like energy', 'ecologic'. I personally do not feel it necessary to define these concepts. In trying to define them, important intuitive meaning may get lost. I believe that the meaning of these concepts will become clear if you allow yourself the opportunity to connect to the ideas without trying to force insight and understanding. The concepts provide the framework in which to look at your performance on the field in a dynamic new way.

The process from the 6th October 1990 to completion of this book has offered me glimpses of clarity in my own thinking. The main driving force throughout my writing was to try and formalise my ideas on mind in sport, so that I am able to share some of my meaning with you. Being a psychotherapist, I also found myself looking at healthy living and the development of meaningful relationships in groups.

Each individual creates his or her own reality of a situation. These concepts are at the core of my own reality in how life functions. Each person can only see the workings of the world through his or her eyes. This book gives you a piece of my reality. I offer these ideas as starting points for further dialogue and not as absolute truths. Truth is beyond words and ideas.

## CHAPTER 1

# Mind in action

Sport offers one the opportunity to experience body and mind in motion. Understanding the body-mind link and the interaction between mind and body during performance is essential to enhance your quality and standard of performance. The focus of this chapter is to examine how the mind operates before and during performance. In order to gain more practical insights into how mind and body interact with each other, I arranged informal discussions with Jimmy Cook (cricket), Bruce Fordyce (ultra-marathon), Brian Mitchell (boxing) and Jonty Rhodes (cricket and hockey). These sportsmen represent a sense of being that goes beyond sport. They have all achieved remarkable heights in their respective sports. Their performances on the field of play offer our youngsters perfect role models.

Sport provides a context where we should learn about ourselves. More importantly, sport can teach us about the 'nature of things'. As our thinking evolves to greater complexity, it is necessary to examine the true nature of sporting competition in our highly competitive and technological society. In particular, it is important to explore how mind operates in such a context.

For example, a conscious determined effort to try and achieve success, may result in failure. The harder you try, the tenser you may become, the less you achieve. In a sense then, the often heard comment from the coach to 'try harder', may inadvertently create more possibility for failure.

Sportsmen are constantly being challenged by their own limited thinking during performance. The challenge to mind surfaces when the athlete feels and believes that he is not achieving the required standards that he has set for himself, or if achievement is not being attained in a time frame that he expects of himself.

Hyams (1982:87) reflects on a story from an anonymous source:

A young boy travelled across Japan to the school of a famous martial artist. When he arrived at the dojo he was given an audience by
the sensei. 'What do you wish from me?' the master asked. 'I wish to
be your student and become the finest karateka in the land', the boy
replied. 'How long must I study?' 'Ten years at least', the master
answered. 'Ten years is a long time', said the boy. 'What if I studied
twice as hard as all your other students?' 'Twenty years', replied the
master. 'Twenty years! What if I practise day and night with all my
effort?' 'Thirty years', was the master's reply. 'How is it that each
time I say I will work harder, you tell me that it will take longer?' the
boy asked. 'The answer is clear. When one eye is fixed upon your
destination, there is only one eye left with which to find the Way.'

## EASTERN PHILOSOPHY

I have found a number of valuable insights in Eastern philosophy
that are able to enhance highly competitive performance. These
concepts are intuitively understood by elite sportsmen and in particular, are seen to operate during children's play. This may seem
somewhat unusual and contradictory, yet highlights the paradoxical nature of peak performance.

The two Eastern wisdoms that lend themselves most to competitive sport are Zen and Taoism. Eastern sport linked to these
philosophies offers the participants a context in which to promote
their own growth and spirituality (Galante, 1981; Hyams, 1982;
Kushner, 1988; Lash, 1989).

I believe that sport performance is riddled with contradictions
and paradox. Zen philosophy can provide some clarity as to how
mind and body interact. The relationship between mind and body
needs to be understood, if there is to be any possibility of natural
and unforced integration. Peak performances only occur when
mind and body integrate and become one.

The central concepts of Taoism will be covered in detail in
Chapter 3. Briefly the philosophy of Taoism is based on the striving
for balance as opposing forces interact in a situation. A dynamic

balance should always exist between opposing forces. This is a fundamental process in natural ecosystems; nothing is maximised or minimised. Instead, there exists a delicate balance of interaction between all elements, ensuring the continuation of the complexity of all life forms.

Taoism also acknowledges the cycles and rhythms of life. The cycle continues. The same concept applies to sport. There are cycles of upward and downward flow. Of central importance, is knowing how to respond to the conditions that prevail. In sporting activity, upward and downward cycles of performance need to be understood and dealt with in ways that will enhance performance. This is at the core of generating powerful energy for performance.

## Religion

There is a misbelief that these philosophies are anti-Christian or anti-Judaic. This concern is examined fully by Father Kadowaki, a Catholic piest, in a deeply thoughtful and insightful book, *Zen and the Bible*. He points out that the way of Zen and true Christian doctrine are very close indeed.

The paradox of living is that one moves closer to death while living each day. In a sense, one is living to die. Looked at it slightly differently, it is through the understanding that death will arrive, that life becomes so precious. One then truly lives each day to its fullest. This is one of the key concepts in all religions and, in particular, is emphasised in Zen training.

Zen and Taoism are not religions. Instead, they are age-old wisdoms originating in the East. The ideas that I use from Zen and Taoism have special relevance in how I believe mind to operate in a sporting context, as well as to understand the cycles or flow in sporting interaction.

Jonty Rhodes, a devout Christian, does not perceive any internal clash of beliefs between his faith and the ideas of Zen and Taoism as I have applied them to sport. In reading further, it is necessary for you to draw your own conclusions and to decide for yourself.

Religious beliefs should not be excluded from the mental preparation of an athlete. An inner peace can be found in prayer or in meditation. Of significance, is that this process of reflection ensures humbleness during sporting achievements. Further, prayer, meditation or quiet reflective thinking are ways to attain understanding and acceptance of experiential difficulties that may arise during sporting performance.

## ZEN

The way of Zen offers the way to examine the paradoxical nature of achievement in competitive sport. Zen is a way of being. Of significance to sport are the aspects of nowness, simplicity of action, passivity of mind or 'no mind', and knowing your limits. These ideas will be discussed in more detail later in the chapter.

A fundamental reason for Zen training is to obtain enlightenment, which if 'aimed' for, cannot ever be achieved. This realisation is actually the enlightenment. In life, there is only a journey. Destinations are only defined in the mind.

> 'Life has a purpose, but a strange purpose. When you come to the end of the road and find perfect insight you will see that enlightenment is a joke' – Zen master. (Van de Wetering, 1987:8)

A further aspect of Zen is the mind's confrontation with a *koan*. (A riddle, the answer to which lies in experience and not logic). A koan is a 'simple' question posed by the master aimed at the student. Its simplicity unfortunately, does not allow for immediate insight. Its effect is to fragment the ego. The task of the student is to become one with his koan. A koan challenges stubborn and resistant thinking. The aim is to stimulate 'no mind' and in the process some enlightenment.

> 'Become one with your koan, forget yourself, forget everything that is connected to you. Sit still, in balance, breathe quietly, destroy everything in your mind. Stay calm and be indifferent to anything which worries you, or seems important, or fascinates' – Zen master. (Van de Wetering, 1987:37)

The road leading to the top is challenging. Athletes are constantly being confronted with difficulties. In discussion with Jimmy Cook regarding his performance in the 1992 Currie Cup cricket season, he felt that he was really playing well, yet did not seem to be making runs. One mistake lead to his dismissal. When asked how he responded to this, he stated that he practised harder and harder. 'On reflection, maybe I was making the same mistakes in the nets, as I was making in the middle,' he commented. This is an interesting point. I believe that when a sportsman confronts a difficulty regarding his performance, a balance between reflective, detached thinking (about the problem) and determined focused action is needed. This balance provides one with new creative insights.

## BECOME THE MOMENT

*Enter the moment,*
*Live the moment,*
*Be the moment,*
*You are the moment.*

> 'As long as what you are doing at the moment is EXACTLY what you are doing at that moment and nothing else, you are one with yourself and with what you are doing – and that is Zen.' (Hyams, 1987:20)

Jonty Rhodes was considered to be somewhat of a surprise selection for the South African World Cup cricket team that toured Australia in 1992. 'The one thing that I set out for myself was to enjoy myself. I didn't know how many games I would play. I thought that I would only play about three or four games, and the rest do 12th man duty. So right at the outset, I decided to enjoy myself as if it was going to be the last game that I played.' These comments highlight the importance of living the moment. Watching Jonty on the field and when batting, it was evident that he was totally committed and involved in what was happening around him. He was an inspiration to his team mates. At the end of the tour, Jonty had captured the attention of the world media. He had become an overnight fielding sensation. At the end of the tour, he had played in all of the World Cup games, including the semi-final test match against England in which he scored a valuable 43 runs (second highest score).

In talking about his omission from the South African squad for the World Cup and the tour to the West Indies, Jimmy Cook stated that he had learnt that things are always changing. 'Nothing can ever be taken for granted. All that you can do is be ready when your chance arrives. I am working hard at my game for that moment. Then we will see if they can leave me out of the team.' Elite sportsmen are masters at being ready for an opportunity.

### Past, Present, Future Focus

It is important to make the distinction between past, present and future focus. Sport operates in the here and now. To become one with the moment implies that you lose yourself in the present. Your energies are released spontaneously without thought or conscious decision. Your movements are smooth. The moment dictates the action, while the action shapes the moment. In the process, the experience of time is not objective. While writing, there have been moments when I lose myself in the typewriter. The keys seem to be working themselves. Time disappears. Surprisingly I do not feel tired. There is energy flow without conscious effort. Now I reflect on what I have written and in my effort to explain further, I am unable to create another sentence. I become stuck. I realise that I am now separate from the moment. Unfortunately, conscious effort to enter nowness prevents ease of flow in action.

> 'Nowness is with us, yet always elusively evading our grasp. Bringing ourselves into the here and now sounds deceptively simple but is essentially very difficult. Other times and moments — traces of the past and shadows of the future — crowd into our awareness of the present moment. Nowness practice does not mean excluding the past and future but an awareness of the subservience of both to the present moment.' (Brandon, 1976:62)

Think of time moving, presenting opportunities in motion. Now 'freeze frame' a moment. As one moves in the moment, energy is being directed into flow and action. The moment has been shaped by past action, and present energy determines the shape of the next moment.

To illustrate this further, think of a cricket match where a contest between bowler and batsman is unfolding. A ball is bowled which hits the batsman on the pads. A loud appeal for L.B.W. (leg before wicket) occurs. 'Not out', says the umpire. For batsman and bowler, this moment is perceived and interpreted very differently. The feelings of these players are different. While the batsman is relieved, the bowler may feel cheated and believe that the batsman is lucky. These feelings now shape the next moment. What sort of ball will be bowled next and how will the batsman respond to the situation?

Feeling anxious about the previous ball and the L.B.W. appeal, the batsman may tighten physically and inwardly worry. This will affect how he will play his next shot. Even a bad ball may be played with excessive caution. The bowler, on the other hand, may feel more confident, and this may result in him bowling another outstanding ball. And so the movement of separate moments over time influence and interact with each other. The batsman needs to forget the previous ball that was bowled, and fully focus his energy and concentration in the present moment (on the ball that is going to be bowled now). The quicker he is able to do this, the more chance he gives himself to truly see and play the next ball for what it really is. If it is a bad ball, he will hit it for four runs. If it is another good ball, he will play defensively.

'Nowness closes no doors. It involves an openness which throws away fears and expectations.' (Brandon, 1976:67)

### No Evaluation during Performance

You should not evaluate performance during performance. As soon as you do, you become past orientated. Present energy becomes dissipated in value judgements. Your present perception will also become clouded by your focus in the situation that has already been.

In his book *Zen and the Art of Motorcycle Maintenance*, Pirsig (1974:247) states that 'reality is always the moment of vision before the intellectualisation takes place'. It is in this moment that the essence of quality exists. Further, Pirsig contends that intellectuals have the greatest trouble seeing quality (they are so swift and absolute about transferring everything into intellectual form). The ones who have the easiest time seeing this quality are children.

Children are always able to connect to a situation without preconceived expectations. They are able to find interest in the most simple things. I once watched my son, aged five, study a spider spinning its web. He sat for hours connected in the process. He had found meaning. He saw quality in the situation. He was engrossed in the moment.

## Creation of Expectations

Expectations and judgements prevent one from operating fully in the moment. The biggest obstacle for relaxed creative performance is focusing on the result. I continually hear from athletes that they want to win. Obviously this is a powerful driving force within, yet it can prevent full awareness in dealing with the demands that present themselves on the field.

Keep action simple. The result will look after itself. I followed (glued to the television) the historic five day test between South Africa and the West Indies, played in Barbados in April 1992. It was our re-entry into test match cricket, after 22 years of isolation.

As I followed the fascinating contest between bat and ball, I became aware of how expectations were being created in the media and on television, as the test match unfolded. I now explore the nature of these expectations, as I perceived them, while sitting in the comfort and safety of my home in South Africa. I share these perceptions with you, without judgement. I wonder how the team was being influenced in their own minds by the comments that were being made in the newspapers and on television. Expectations and judgements that are created by others tend to interfere with one's own relaxed performance.

At the end of the third day the position of the match was West Indies 1st innings 262, South Africa 1st innings 345, and the West Indies 2nd innings 184 for 7 wickets. At this stage the West Indies were 101 runs ahead, with 3 wickets standing. To add further 'comfort', those remaining 3 wickets were previously taken for only 12 runs in the 1st innings. *The Star* Tuesday April 21 1992 reads: 'SA on brink of test victory'. However, Robert Houwing in the same paper writes: 'Still a big job to do in Bridgetown...Kepler issues warning note'.

The television commentators start to create the reality that if South Africa can get the remaining wickets for not more than another 50 runs, victory will be achieved. Watching the television, I wonder what 'dialogue' had occurred between the pressmen/television commentators, and the players at the end of that third day? Creating expectations of end targets, can trap or restrict creative thinking. Nevertheless, the discussion and commentary on television leads the viewer into assuming that a 2nd innings batting target of 150 runs is what South Africa should aim for. For some unknown reason it has been decided that 150 runs is the target; who and how this has been decided is not known, but an expectation has been created.

The morning session of the fourth day conjures up remarkable, unpredictable cricket. From the body language of the South African fielders and bowlers, it is apparent that the flow of activity is not going according to pre-determined plans. The commentators are also becoming despondent. Catches are dropped. Stress increases. Everbody has forgotten the moment. The tension and frustration builds. Energy flow is being distracted and disrupted as the expected target of 150 runs arrives and vanishes. In the process, a feeling of disappointment seems to emerge.

The West Indies eventually are all out for 283 (99 runs were added to the overnight score), leaving the South Africans needing 201 to win. At the end of play on the 4th day the score reads: South Africa 122 for 2 , with Kepler Wessels 74 and Peter Kirsten 36, both not out. There are only 79 runs needed for a win and there are still 8 wickets standing. *The Star* Thursday April 23 reads: 'Wessels poised to shape victory'. The front page article states: 'Kepler leads charge for historic victory'. I now inwardly wish that that word 'victory' could be banned from thinking. It creates traps in the mind. Unfortunately, our minds are masters at judgement and expectation in reality creating.

I reflect again and think that the only way out of the limitations of the thinking ahead is to lose oneself in the moment. 'Hum a song

while batting or focus on your breathing,' is the advice that I shout
out to the television. It is obviously aimed at our batsmen. I find
myself feeling so helpless as the events unfold. 'Let your spontaneous energy flow without looking at the score board. Seize the
moment. More importantly, enjoy the moment. Do not push ahead,
forgetting to hold your bat in your hand. Do not get excited at what
might be, without watching the ball being bowled,' I plead, again
talking to the television.

*The Star* Friday April 24 reads: 'It's collapso cricket as SA batsmen capitulate'. Robert Houwing of *The Star* writes: 'Put it down to
inexperience'. The article on the front page states: 'Fifth day proved
a bridge too far'. The South African second innings had ended at
148 all out. The last 8 wickets had fallen for 26 runs. Even the target
of only having to get 150 runs for the second innings that was initially thought as being within the capabilities of the South African
batsmen would have resulted in a 2 run loss. It was truly remarkable how at the end of the 3rd day, a rigid mind-set had been
unconsciously programmed.

Jimmy Cook contends that the batsmen tightened in the
moment due to inexperience. 'Our batsmen became timid. Instead
of attacking, we thought that we had all day to get the 79 runs.
Losing Kepler so soon didn't do us any good. We became defensive. Also, we tended to look for things in the pitch, instead of just
playing each ball as it came. If you get bowled due to one keeping
low, there is nothing you can do about it. But it is fatal for a batsman to be reading too much in the pitch.' Playing each ball as it
comes, without looking for anything in the pitch, or expecting a
possible deviation, suggests that each ball presents a unique
moment for the batsman to deal with. It becomes important to shut
out the previous ball that was bowled, to forget about the score or
runs to be made; and to direct all the intense concentration in the
moment.

## *Enjoy the Moment*

In the build-up to the 1990 Currie Cup rugby final, the Natal players developed the chirp: 'Enjoy the moment'. They had realised

that playing in the final was a special rugby moment. They were, therefore, determined to enjoy everything that they had to deal with, even the might of the Northern Transvaal forwards. The exact composition of the side would never be the same again. Each individual player had a unique opportunity to prove some-thing to himself during the challenge of a Currie Cup final. It was important for each player to realise that here was a moment in his own rugby career, waiting to be lived. The decision was his.

## NO MIND

In his book *On Having No Head*, Harding (1986:1) gives a vivid account of an experience in the Himalayas. It was simple. He stopped thinking. Reason and internal chatter died down. 'There existed only the Now, that present moment and what was clearly given in it.'

In Zen, there is a state of mind referred to as *mushin*. Mushin is a state in which one is consciously unconscious and unconsciously conscious (Kushner, 1988: 41). During sports performance you do not want to be thinking too much. Bruce Fordyce believes that sport is an art and not a science. He feels that too much planning, too much intensity, and trying to be in control and anticipate all possibilities interferes with the natural flow in one's body.

Zen practice attempts to achieve the state of 'no mind' in medi-tation. In kyudo (Zen archery), the state of mushin can be attained through the integration of breathing, concentration and posture (Kushner, 1988). I have found that going on a long-distance run provides that same experience for me. Firstly, if I feel stressed and overwhelmed with mental pressure, I am able to calm my mind if I physically become active (run). In the process of running, I notice that a quietness emerges. Then there are intermittent creative ideas that surface. After some exploration, I find myself just running without thought. The phenomenon of focus and flow arises. During the focus phase, one entertains a specific thought. As time moves on, there are no other ideas. You lose yourself in the run-ning. This is the flow.

### Relaxed Concentration

I am often asked by athletes on ways to improve concentration. I believe that the phenomenon of concentration is misunderstood. 'No mind' is actually the period of relaxed, unforced concentration, which occurs when mind and body integrate. It is worth mentioning that concentration is not the mind telling the mind to concentrate. This is forced prescription. Concentration is not forced thinking.

I was once consulted by the parents of a four year old, with the complaint that the child never wanted to listen. In discussion, the parents outlined that when the child was playing, they were unable to get her to respond to their demands or requests. They had taken her for a hearing test that revealed perfect hearing. With further exploration of the problem, it became clear that this child had the ability to cocoon herself in silence during play. There were no distractions or interference, since she had lost herself in play.

In highly competitive sport a state of mushin can be achieved. After the Currie Cup final against Northern Transvaal, some of the Natal players' comments reflected that they had attained a state of mushin. 'Did you hear the crowd screaming?' Response: 'What crowd?' 'Was it hot?' Response: 'I don't recall.'

The mind often gets bored with the demands on the field if one is not connected to the process or flow of activity. If you are connected to the flow, the mind gets 'lost'. It responds without thought.

### Stop the Internal Noise

Self-talk or internal chatter on the field reflects an activity of mind. Gallwey contends that sportsmen should learn how to 'quieten the mind'. In order to explore this concept of a quiet mind, Gallwey (1976:18) makes the distinction between Self 1 and Self 2. In a sense, this is a distinction between ego (or mind) and body. Self 1 is like a parent. It is the logical, analytical part of self that always has an answer to the situation. It is the teller. Self 2 is the performer. It always tries its best. This is important to remember. I have yet to come across a sportsman who deliberately goes out of his way to make mistakes.

Activity between Self 1 and Self 2 uses up vital internal energy that should be expended in actual play. Disruption and dissipation of available energy occurs due to the internal dialogue between fragmented parts of the self. This activity usually erupts when the athlete has made a mistake, and the ego (mind) starts blaming the body for not performing to standard. The mind then becomes hooked on the past mistake; and in its quest to 'help' the body, prescribes the necessary activity for future action. The performer (Self 2) is now caught between two conflicting energy sappers. Part of the self is repentant (past focus), while another part of the self looks ahead (future focus) in order to redeem itself.

Gallwey believes that it is necessary to let go of your judgements. In a sense, this implies that you become unconditional and detached during play. The eminent psychologist, Carl Rogers (1967), contends that unconditional acceptance is the most powerful ingredient in creating a context in which meaningful relationships can be developed. In essence, this unconditional acceptance of one's own self is at the core of attaining a quiet, calm mind. Having no conditions allows one the freedom to be creative, or simply the freedom to be.

'No mind' should not be confused with a state where you are unable to make decisions on the field. Nothing can be further from the true nature of a quiet mind.

> 'The mind of a perfect man is like a mirror. It grasps nothing. It expects nothing. It reflects but does not hold. Therefore, the perfect man can act without effort.' (Chuang-Tzu, quoted in Hyams, 1982:101)

Jonty Rhodes contends that the thought processes in sport are so quick there is no time to think. When asked why he dived in that sensational run-out of Inzamam-ul-Haq that changed the course of the World Cup test match against Pakistan he replied, 'I don't know. I just responded.'

International athletes in highly interactive sports need to be able to function under stress, in reduced interactional space, and under extreme time pressure. In rugby, hockey and soccer, for example, space and time are the two factors that distinguish international sporting demands from ordinary club or provincial demands. The actual sport does not change.

Decision-making under stress (due to the pressures of reduced space and time), requires an aspect of 'no mind' to be present. In other words, the ability to make a decision without actually thinking becomes the essence of how elite sportsmen function. In the first place, this becomes possible if the body has been put through sufficient exhaustive training. This is necessary since a tired body does not allow for spontaneous and creative thinking. 'When the legs go, the mind goes'. Further, the ability to become aware of the possibilities of potential passing options without the ball allows the mind to be one or two steps ahead of the interaction. On receiving the ball, the 'thinking' has to some extent already occurred. Now one trusts in the mind-body harmony and oneness that occurs in that given moment with the ball. Decisions are made without conscious thought.

Golfers are faced with the exact opposite problem concerning the attainment of 'no mind'. Golf is a sport that offers the greatest challenge to obtaining a clear, calm mind. The reason is quite simple: there is too much time to think. Golfers always play two games of golf in a round. The 'game' between shots while walking to the ball (this is played in the mind); and then the actual game of hitting the ball. Golfers need to be able to clear their minds before hitting the ball. Active thought during a shot disrupts energy flow, and also blocks out awareness.

In consulting with golfers, I suggest that they follow a routine that ensures a balance between thinking and 'no thinking'. After teeing off, the task of the mind should be to detach from judging the shot and instead become aware of external (outside of yourself) and internal (inside yourself) information that exists in the situation. Contacting the environment is important. Awareness of vegetation, of the types of trees, the existence of the different colours and the mood of fellow players. Internal information regarding self includes breathing pattern, bodily tensions, pace of walking, manner of talking, thought patterns and ideas that are occupying mind.

This awareness provides the opportunity for your mind to take in much information on a conscious level about how you operate in the situation. While walking to the ball, a period of 'no thinking' will spontaneously occur. There may be moments when you are just walking. There are no thoughts, no plans. Further, the mind may drift off and involve itself with other ideas or thoughts unrelated to golf, or you may become involved and lose yourself in some conversation with a fellow golfer.

As you now approach the ball, the mind starts narrowing its focus so that you can make a decision on what club to use and what shot to play. On reaching the ball, a unique shot needs to be played. The mind has consciously gathered information. As you make the decision on the shot you intend playing, you are in thinking mode. Now step back from the ball and visualise yourself hitting the ball exactly as you have decided. In your mind's eye, see and feel yourself hitting the ball.

After this process, stand next to the ball and physically practise and go through the shot that you intend to play. This helps in grooving the swing and the body movement. Become aware of the feel. After this practice, address the ball in order to now play the shot. Remain focused on the feel. As the shot is being played, you should be in a state of 'no thinking'. You trust your body rhythm to execute the shot that you had planned for and visualised.

## REMAIN SIMPLE IN THE JOURNEY

It has been said that life is so simple that we cannot understand it. Modern life is fast and demanding. Competition is high. Striving for success is at the core of most of our thinking. The definition of success varies, yet it is invariably linked to materialistic possessions or achieving a defined goal. In sport, success is winning. Winning offers a feeling of wellbeing to sportsmen. It becomes linked to one's self-concept.

A translation from the *Tao Te Ching* offers wisdom:

'See simplicity in the complicated
Achieve greatness in little things.' (Lash, 1989:115, Verse 63)

During actual performance remain simple in your actions. This provides a secure platform and foundation from which to launch performance. During periods of stress and distraction, focus on simple action. Elite sportsmen tend to become too complex in the execution of tasks. Some have lost interest in simplicity. However, it is simplicity that frees you from false values. Further, it is from simplicity that creative energy flows. New action grows spontaneously from a thoroughness in simplicity.

It is necessary to 'groove' the body for action. The body must learn what it feels like during the execution of certain tasks. In the process muscle memory is enhanced which allows the state of 'no mind' to occur. The grooving of the body requires repetitive execution of a task. Repetition in action can become boring, yet is necessary in order to reach a level of being (or 'no mind') during competitive action. The process of 'grooving' the execution of simple action is the foundation of success.

Top athletes will practise the same skill over and over again. The one objective should be to maintain a consistently high standard and quality of task execution. Even when a high level of performance has been achieved, further 'grooving' should continue in order to challenge the mind to remain focused on the simple execution of the same task over and over again.

### Too Much Thinking Causes Concern

When the mind has time to build up expectations it can inadvertently block certain action. My son, aged 11 years, was constantly complaining about a small growth on his arm, yet had built up expectations of the possible pain of its removal by the doctor. In all of the emotional family discussion, no time was ever set for the visit to the doctor. An appointment in advance would have proved to be emotionally draining for him. Knowing that the day was drawing closer and closer would have heightened his mind's creation of more and more possibilities of horrific medical treatment.

Every conceivable possibility of what the doctor was likely to do, was entertained in my son's mind during family discussion regarding the growth. In the process, he became more and more reluctant to visit the doctor.

Quite spontaneously, my wife telephoned the doctor and managed to get an appointment on that very same day. The appointment fitted in immediately after my son's football match. With no time to think, with no time to intellectualise, he found himself having to deal with an unexpected and unplanned event. He was now in the actual situation without the build-up of anticipated possibilities. He was now required to deal with the situation as it actually unfolded in the doctor's surgery. He really surprised himself in how well he coped. In discussion afterwards, he remarked to me that he felt that he had made a big complicated issue out of a very simple problem.

The success of Natal winning the 1990 Currie Cup final against Northern Transvaal at Loftus Versfeld had at its core, simplicity. On a psychological level there were a number of obstacles confronting the side. The experience of the Northern Transvaal team, the highly respected tradition of Northern Transvaal rugby, playing at Loftus Versfeld, the genius of Naas Botha, the fact that Natal had only been in two previous Currie Cup finals, and the fact that Natal had already experienced two heavy defeats from Northern Transvaal in the league matches of that season. Further, historically Natal had only previously beaten Northern Transvaal on two occasions in Currie Cup matches. These issues all present a complicated maze of psychological concerns. If the mind entertains these thoughts, a web of uncertainty and doubt is spun. How is it possible to transcend this complexity and still remain simple in outlook?

The more complex the problem, the more simple one should become in action.

The mind needs to make a choice in situations like this. Does it focus on the psychological complexity and entertain thoughts about the past history as I have outlined, or do the players focus on achieving simple goals on the field of play? Under stress, the mind tends to lose focus. It is during these periods that the mind starts entertaining irrelevant ideas. In the process, energies become diffused. So, it was imperative that the players were able to maintain focus on simple achievable goals and understand how these simple goals connected to each other. In this way the team would become more directed and powerful. Further, the focus was to be on what each of the players wanted to achieve, as opposed to worrying about what Northern Transvaal were going to do.

In talking about the stress leading up to an important race, Bruce Fordyce concerns himself only with getting himself physically and psychologically ready for the race. 'There are a lot of rumours circulating around before a race. I have learnt that there may be 20 runners on the day who are going to be red hot. I must just make sure that I am ready and all right.' Bruce becomes more internal, and makes sure that he has prepared to the best of his own ability. He leaves nothing to chance regarding his own preparation. It is important not to use energy worrying about others. You have no control over what they are doing. But you do have control about how you are thinking about them.

### More to Offer?

It was interesting to see how those who had made contact with me, after Natal's success, expected me to reveal major complicated techniques of the 'success formula'. After my involvement with Natal, I was approached for help by a rugby club side who were going to play in a promotion/relegation final. After some discussion with the players, I sensed that the players seemed disappointed with what we were talking about. I was trying to get to understand what the players believed were their strengths. I was emphasising the importance of the execution of perfectly simple basics during the match. 'The trap is to think that this game is different,' I stated.

The players did not seem comfortable with this comment. There was a belief that there was more to the success package. In the minds of the players, it seemed that the final needed to be approached differently. This belief provided the necessary food for thought that energised the players into confronting their own expectations regarding the final. Is the final really different from other matches? If so, what would the main difference be? During the discussion, the players were able to make a distinction between actual match demands (these were exactly the same as for other matches); and the importance of the club being promoted into a premier division. The importance of the match had increased the stress levels of the players, as well as implying that it might be necessary to change a winning formula that the club had developed over the season. In fact, I stated that the players should reflect on the reasons why they had achieved so much during the season. As the discussion unfolded it emerged that the team played 'simple, direct, fast' rugby. This needed to be re-emphasised, not changed.

Jimmy Cook has a set mental map when going out to bat. He contends that the first 20 minutes require intense concentration. In this period, he gets a feel for the ball, and the pace and bounce of the wicket. He is not trying to score runs. Instead, his focus is on achieving the simple goal of getting in touch with his environment. 'You don't want to get too clever in the beginning,' says Jimmy.

Meaningful experiences occur when a sportsman is able to get excited in the simplicity of the journey. There is no focus on the destination. Instead, the mind becomes aware of how simple it really is. It does not try and create extra demands in order to entertain itself. Instead, the athlete remains focused on the execution of a simple goal. Once achieved, creative flow in performance follows. During the flow, there is not much thinking. A feeling of 'no mind' is experienced.

## REALISE YOUR LIMITS

An athlete matures over time. This process involves understanding and accepting your strengths and weaknesses during performance. Players who play to their own strengths, and avoid trying to do those things that increase the possibility of exposing their weaknesses, perform more consistently over time.

This creates a feeling of comfortableness in what you are doing. It provides the necessary security. This comfort promotes further learning. The trap is to believe that you have to be perfect at everything that you do. This is an impossibility. Instead, work at perfecting those aspects of your game that you are capable of doing. The difficulty is deciding which actions make up your strengths, as opposed to those actions that put you most at risk during your performance.

### No Satisfaction in Comparison

Most people are not truly satisfied with who they are or what they have got. There is a restlessness in us that drives us to try and achieve more and more. In interaction with others, we continually compare ourselves to them. This is the core of the materialistic world that we live in. There is very little inner contentment.

One imagines a top sportsman to be perfect. Nothing could be further from the truth. Instead, a top athlete needs to know his own strengths and weaknesses; and then operate in such a way as to enhance his strengths and nullify his weaknesses. From the discussions with Jimmy Cook and Jonty Rhodes, it appears that there is a definite thought pattern in eventually reaching the point where one is aware of one's own limits. Jimmy commented that when Graeme Pollock moved up to the Transvaal from Eastern Province, he found himself trying to bat like Graeme. 'The biggest turning point in my career was when Graeme came to Transvaal. When we saw him bat, I thought that that was the way to play. You have to smack the ball around like Graeme does. And it took me a month, and I thought to myself: "Hang on a second, I must be mad to try and bat like that. Let me bat like I can bat, let me do what I can do. I know what's good for me, and I know what stimulates me to play, and let me do that." I think I took a big turn then. You cannot bat like Graeme, he is a genius.'

In discussing his hockey performance, Jonty commented: 'As long as I focus on not trying to get too clever, and instead go with what I can do naturally, I never force the issue. I realise that I have my limits. Everyone has their limits. If you play within your limits you will never force the issue. In the early stages of my hockey career, I tried to be like Trevor Madsen (ex South African hockey forward who played for Natal). It took me a year to realise that I am not a Trevor Madsen. What is good for Trevor is not necessarily good for Jonty Rhodes. And what is good for Jonty Rhodes, is what is going to work. As long as I play within that, I will be all right.' 'Do you think a person can become great if he understands what his limits are?' I asked. 'I think that that is the most important thing in becoming great,' replied Jonty.

### Accept Yourself

In order to know your limits, it appears that one first compares oneself to a role model. This is natural. As you try and emulate this person, you strive to improve and become better. However, there comes a point in time when the successful athlete takes a step back and looks carefully at his own abilities. Jonty expands further, 'You have to go out and experience to realise your limitations for a start. The quicker you realise, the more successful you will become.' 'What's going to make you realise?' I enquired. 'You need to experience the bad times. If you are winning all the time, you take things for granted.' Jonty then outlined his difficulties experienced in his second year of Currie Cup cricket. 'Once you know what it's like down at the bottom, you don't ever want to go down there again.'

In order to confront your limitations, it may be necessary for you to experience difficulties during performance. These problems are in a sense, important messages to which the athlete needs to listen. The 'downs' are telling the athlete to become one with himself, and realise his limits. It becomes a time for learning. Successful sportsmen are acutely aware of their strengths and weaknesses.

Awareness of oneself, and knowing oneself are prerequisites to acceptance of oneself. This becomes a maturation process. Through experience, the athlete starts becoming aware of his feelings and behaviours in the build-up to competition. Further, his awareness of himself in action also increases. This process leads to the athlete gaining a deeper understanding of himself. His knowledge of himself provides the necessary information for achievement. He now needs to learn how to use this knowledge to his best advantage.

Once the athlete has reached this level, an acceptance of self is at the core of his action. Knowing your strengths and then being able to play to your strengths, reduces the chances of failure. Alternatively, the ability to not get yourself into situations where your limitations are exposed, is in line with the adage 'Prevention is better than cure'.

I was fortunate to have played both provincial cricket and hockey. My selections, however, came at the rather old age of 28 years old. I did not perceive myself as being highly talented. Yet, I was not afraid of hard physical work. I also had the ability to persevere during my training. While playing hockey for Transvaal, I knew that my stick work was limited and that I would expose myself if I tried to dribble and hold onto the ball for too long. My strengths were my basic skills of stopping and hitting, as well as my marking and tackling ability. Throughout my provincial hockey career, I focused on not exposing my weaknesses. I maintained simplicity in making passes, and based my play on the perfected technique of hitting and stopping. I eliminated the need to dribble the ball. As I gained more and more experience, the matches became easier. Not because I had become a better and better player; but rather due to my acceptance of my strengths and limitations. I had refrained from becoming over-confident and complacent as my performance improved, since I understood that my success was only due to my focus on the perfection of simple basics. This was my strength. If the improvement and confidence in my play had lead me into believing that it was now possible to dribble around opponents, I have no doubt that within a couple of matches my performance would have dropped severely.

## SPORTING DIFFICULTIES

Sport is full of challenges. As you involve yourself in sporting activity, the overcoming of both physical and mental obstacles ensures higher level development. This is the nature of sporting progress. In order to overcome both physical and mental difficulties, the athlete will discover that it is necessary to introduce some newness in training or in thinking. The reason for this, is that difficulties are invariably caused by the repetition of the same mistakes over time. Being creatures of pattern and routine, the difficulty usually activates that familiar parental piece of advice in the inner mind: 'If you don't succeed, try, try and try again'. In the process, the difficulty grows in size and stature. A resistant wall that blocks progress may emerge.

As you try and break through the difficulty, become aware of whether you are winning the battle. Dedicated commitment in practice becomes a necessary ingredient in resolving difficulties, but with a new added axiom: 'If you don't succeed after trying, try something slightly different'. A difficulty should start eroding over time, if you are utilising your efforts and knowledge in the correct way.

All sportsmen have experienced sporting difficulties that are resistant to change. Zen recommends that you become one with your difficulty. Ask yourself what the problem is trying to teach you about yourself or the situation you find yourself in. On a deeper level, the problem may be trying to teach you something about life. Meditate on this. Take a quiet moment during relaxation to reflect on the difficulty that you are experiencing. Do not try and anxiously find a solution. Instead, become one with your sporting koan. Sport should never be separated from life. The true value of sport is to teach you about the nature of life.

Become one with your difficulty. Try and enter the inner core of what your sport can teach you. Connect to those elements in the sport that test and challenge your body and mind. There should be no force to find solutions. No prescription to achieve understanding. Instead, an acceptance of your predicament is necessary.

It is during the difficult periods that sportsmen are confronted by their own limited and restrictive thinking. In addition, there are possibilities for spiritual development during these phases. The athlete comes to understand his innermost feelings when he is not achieving the success that he has come to expect. During these periods, a humbleness usually results.

Being a Christian, Jonty Rhodes states that he has given his life to the Lord. 'It is not in my hands in what happens. It is a growing experience. If I am going through a bad patch, maybe I have become too arrogant. The Lord works in funny ways.' Jonty has come to understand and appreciate that sport is constantly teaching us things about ourselves, in particular, and about life, in general.

Each athlete has the opportunity to grow spiritually. It only takes the inner desire to open up to the new learning that presents itself. This learning usually takes place, when the athlete is 'down'.

### Listen to Your Body Message

When a person has a problem to deal with, the body emits a 'felt sense' (Gendlin, 1981: 32). A felt sense is not a mental experience, but a physical bodily awareness of a situation, event or person.

Gendlin outlines a process, which he calls focusing, in which one gets in touch with this felt sense. In this way, one is able to unlock the wisdom of the body.

Of interest to sport, is that any problem will manifest itself in a bodily sensation. It may only show itself as an uncomfortableness or uneasiness in the body.This will in turn, restrict the flow of relaxed body movement in space. Of significance, this body sensation will hinder ease of action on the field of play. In the process, tightening within the body will occur which will affect the execution of skills.

It is necessary to create a quiet context so that the mind can connect to this felt sense of the body. While sitting quietly, ask your mind to connect to the felt sense in the body that your sporting difficulty may be causing. Locate the exact place in the body where this feeling exists. A mind-body link becomes the objective. Your body needs to be acknowledged. Its message needs to be heard. This view contends that the body can become a vehicle for changing one's attitude to a problem. The change requires listening to the body sensation, and then linking this sensation to a phrase or image of the problem that you are experiencing. If one approaches this correctly, without force to seek a solution, the felt sense will shift. It will change as you connect with the bodily awareness. When the felt sense changes, you change.

## MIND IN WRITING

At this moment, I would like to reflect on my own experiences of my writing performance. Writing and playing rugby or cricket have many similarities when it comes to the workings of 'mind'. While writing, I have been fortunate that the flow of ideas has occurred rather easily. Unconsciously, I have been writing this book since October 1990 (after my involvement with the Natal rugby team in the 1990 Currie Cup final).

As I reflect inwards, I note that the actual writing to date has taken just over four weeks. My usual work consultations with clients have continued in this period. My normal working pattern has not changed. I have been writing in those periods of quietness.

I was getting excited by the progress that I was making, and then I experienced the feeling of hitting the wall. I was unable to write for a whole week due to work commitments, and over the week-end I was confronted with family commitments. There was a punctuation in my activity flow.

On Sunday night, there was a terrible uneasiness in my stomach (felt sense). I knew that I was having to deal with my disappointment and frustration at not having been able to write during the past week.

Eventually, Monday arrived. The day had been planned for writing. I had great expectations that I was going to produce at least seven pages of meaningful information. I was at last free to write. An interesting thing happened during that day. I only managed a page of writing that I was not personally satisfied with. Intense internal panic set in. I was extremely frustrated. I was deepening the downward flow. I was going against the grain in some way. I was now forced into non-action, when I was actually desperate for high-level competitive action. That night I had to confront myself.

The first thing that I discovered was that you cannot rush the process. I fell into the trap of trying to achieve seven pages of writing, and forgot to enter the moment and re-connect with what I had written the week previously. I increased my own panic because I saw that I was not achieving my goal. I was trying to reach a destination without journeying.

Secondly, I had tried to make up for lost time. I was being governed by the built-up pressure over the past week. Past was encroaching on the 'nowness'.

Thirdly, I had become unbalanced. I find that long-distance running (physical activity) seems to stimulate my mental energy creativity. I had last run over ten days ago. My mind and body were no longer in dynamic harmony. I had unintentionally gone against my own natural rhythm and flow.

Fourthly, I needed to achieve an inward balance before I could proceed further. Hitting the wall was nature's way of showing me that I was interfering with the normal and natural process of writing. My expectations and determined intentions to succeed had stood in my way. They had unbalanced and over-extended me psychologically. Achieving inward balance is often obtained when you are able to detach yourself from the desperation to achieve.

Finally, I also got in touch with the real reason for my panic when my wife asked me a simple question. 'Why is it so important for you to complete this book?'

This verse from the *Tao Te Ching* reflected my internal panic:

'Great success, like disgrace,
Can bring great trouble.
Success which advances ego
Can make you lose your way.' (Dreyer, 1990:112)

My ego had got in the way. I wanted to succeed. I wanted to complete the book quicker than was humanly possible. After some dialogue with my wife, I was able to understand the situation that I had found myself in. I felt relieved and free. My performance proved to be far easier going on Tuesday. I was back in the flow.

## BEYOND TECHNIQUE

Mind in action has mapped out ideas of how you could lose yourself in the activity that unfolds on the sports field. Too much thinking, tends to block the creative flow in body movement. While planning and thinking needs to occur during a match, it is important that one maintains a balance between thinking and 'no thinking'.

Execution of some sporting acts requires complex body movements. I am always amazed at what gymnasts and ice skaters are able to do with their bodies during performance. I believe that these acts can only be executed if the mind is quiet and calm. The paradox (contradiction) regarding sports performance is that when the mind tries to help the body to perform, it may inadvertently interrupt the rhythm of body movement.

I believe that 'being the moment' should have the added axiom of; 'enjoy the moment'. When you do things that you enjoy, you will naturally become one with that activity. You and the activity merge together without effort. All your energy is directed into what you are doing, without force.

I was hitting some practice golf balls with my 7 iron. While hitting the balls, I was trying to get in touch with a certain feel/body sensation that I was experiencing in my arm during the swing. I had laid out about 20 balls, and non-thinkingly moved from ball to ball as I took my stance, got balanced, watched the ball, back-swing, down-swing and hit. In the process, my mind was trying to connect to the body sensation in my arm as the club moved up and then down, making contact with the ball. I was not interested in where the balls were landing. After hitting about 10 or so balls, I stopped the process. To my surprise, I noticed that all the balls were in about a five-metre radius of each other. This was remark-able for a golfer of my handicap. This excited me. As I took up my stance to hit the next ball, I had unconsciously changed my think-ing pattern. I now wanted to hit the ball into this target area. The more I tried to achieve this, the more I failed. I could feel my own frustration building up. I now started to become more determined to succeed. This made things worse.

In the process, I could feel that my mind had set up a competi-tive challenge. I had experienced the disruptive nature of my mind interfering, while out practising hitting golf balls. The idea of 'no mind' made a great deal of sense to me on that day. Having said this, I do believe that your mind has a vital part to play in enchanc-ing your level of performance. It should help in the planning and strategising of activity. But it should not over-prescribe how things should be done and what the end result should be. Maintaining simplicity in the process reminds the athlete to take one step at a time. Running and finishing the Comrades marathon is dependent on each step an athlete takes. Trip on one simple stride, and then you will fall. Reaching your destination requires travelling safely and simply. Do not rush. Do not try and get too clever.

While hitting those golf balls, I also did not realise what my lim-itations were. Once I had decided to try and hit every ball into the target area, I was expecting that I could execute shots like all those professionals do with such ease. I started to put pressure on myself. I had forgotten my own limitations. In the process, I increased the possibility of my own downfall.

Proper mental preparation is a way of being. There are no real techniques. Most of the ideas that I have shared are not new. While the mind may understand some of the concepts, the difficulty is in the implementation. The paradox is that by trying to implement them consciously, one may block spontaneous and creative energy flow.

There is no one right way when it comes to mental preparation. For some athletes, this is of concern, since there is a belief that a magic formula exists. For other athletes, the knowledge that mental preparation is not a specific set plan of action is a freeing experience. What works, should be used. A sportsman matures with experience. In the process, learn about yourself.

## CHAPTER 2

# The psychology of winning

Everyone wants to be a winner. Being a winner in sport is often defined in an extremely ruthless manner. Achieving the gold medal at the end of the race becomes the sole focus of the media, the public, the coach and the players. In working with top sportsmen, I am only too aware of the definite distinction between being a winner and being a loser in the eyes of the public and media. I, for one, do not believe that this can or should be changed. There is something special in winning a final. The experience of overcoming all the physical and mental obstacles during an intense competitive battle against your opponent, is the nature of true sport. However, I do feel that the psychology of winning needs to be broadened. Being a winner transcends actual winning. Therefore, the psychology of winning must go beyond the narrow definition of the end result of winning.

There are a number of techniques and programmes that claim to offer an individual the necessary motivation to win. These programmes often originate from the rules of mechologic (to be outlined in detail in Chapter 4). Specifically, these techniques imply that external motivation can be given into an 'empty vessel'. If you 'drink', then a change in mind will occur. Literature abounds with methods on how to improve one's self-image and achieve the success that you may desire. Success motivation and winning are often outlined in 10-point plans. If you do this, then you will achieve that. Think positive, and you will always succeed. All these recipes and formulae make rational sense, yet often fall down at the times when they are most needed. Why, you may ask? The answer is not easy to establish. I feel that it may be due to not having really understood how mind operates in action.

The mind does not need external prescription. Instead, the mind needs to reflect into itself in a way that allows freedom for action. I also believe that 10-step success motivation techniques are one-sided in only positiveness. This positiveness can often make one feel inadequate. It prescribes certain standards that you need to achieve. This over-extension on positives goes against the fundamentals of ecologic (to be outlined in Chapter 4). Comments about positives imply covert statements about the negatives. 'Think positive' inadvertently tells the mind to stop thinking negatively. The mind, functioning as it does, will then set up an internal battle between positive thoughts (which have been judged to be OK) and negative thoughts (which will result in guilt and remorse since they are not OK). This takes up a great deal of psychic energy.

Bruce Fordyce, Jimmy Cook, Brian Mitchell and Jonty Rhodes are all winners. In commenting about their success on the sports field, all of them acknowledged that they had the necessary talent. Given this, however, all of them attributed their success to hard work and dedication. Jonty believed that 'too many talented people take things for granted'. Bruce's comment about the Comrades is a wonderful metaphor: 'It's a really tough race. You must be mentally prepared for an uphill battle.'

Having acknowledged that discipline and dedication was necessary, there was a further belief that contributed to their success. In all of their comments, there existed a dynamic balance between having fun, enjoyment, and the intensity to do well. There was an inner drive and desire to achieve a high quality of performance, coupled with enjoyment. Bruce believes that youngsters need to try a lot of different sports and not to focus on one too early. 'All the people who I was with at school who were very intense, have now given up. I was never that intense at school. When you have found the one sport that you really like then go for it. Don't pursue things that people tell you to do. Pursue the things that you find to be good fun. If you do it hard enough and well enough, you'll get to the top.' Jonty states that youngsters should have a smile on their face while performing. 'Not even winning is worth not enjoying yourself,' he said. Jimmy felt that if parents put too much pressure on their children too early, they would eventually drop out. 'Parents must let children be children. It is always easy for parents, standing on the side of the field, to shout at their eight year old playing soccer if he makes a mistake. But children learn by making mistakes. Anyway, an eight year old cannot even really kick a ball properly.'

## A CULTURE OF EXCELLENCE

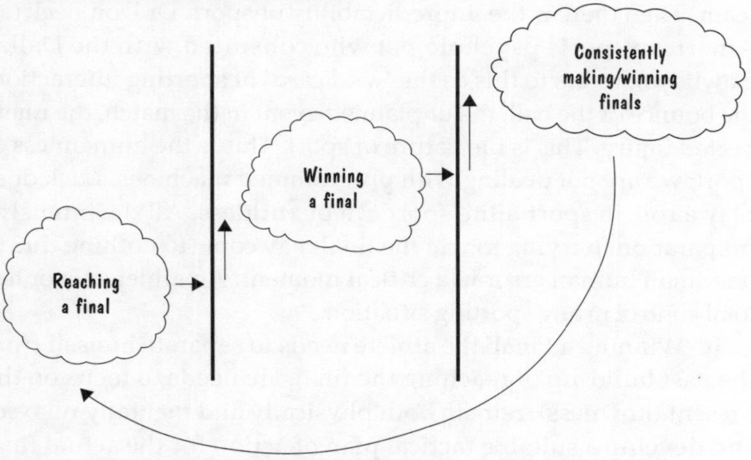

*Figure 1: Creating a culture of excellence*

Figure 1 makes distinctions between Reaching a Final; Winning a Final; and Consistently Making/Winning Finals. Each of these distinctions requires further discussion. For any team or athlete to reach a final, a great deal of committed effort is required during practice. There are no short cuts. Dedication in training requires that an attitude of 'when the going gets tough, the tough get going' be inculcated in mind. Linked to this, is that the athlete needs to be a consistent performer over time. In order to reach the rugby Currie Cup final, for example, the two finalists need to produce high standards of play throughout the season. Ten gruelling matches need to be played. Ten hurdles need to be overcome. 'Reaching a Final' is a metaphor for the long haul of consistent achievement over time. Although reaching a final suggests that a destination has been reached (it has on one level); it also means that another unique journey on the actual final day needs to occur in order to jump to the next level of 'Winning a Final'. The psychology of winning now starts taking on more complexity.

Once having reached the final, a quantum leap in thinking needs to occur on the actual day of the match or event. Some teams have been able to reach finals time and time again, yet never manage to win. History may trap them. Further, too much desperation on the actual day can inadvertently work against the athlete or team. Then there is the unpredictability of sport. Dr Don Beck (an American sports psychologist who consulted with the Dallas Cowboys), refers to this as the 'wild card' of sporting interaction: the bounce of the ball, the unplanned event in the match, the unexpected injury. This is the nature of sport. This is the humanness of sport; we are not dealing with programmed machines. Luck does play a role in sport. Elite sport can be ruthless. All the intensive preparation in trying to win the final may come to nothing due to one small human error in a critical moment. An athlete never has total control in any sporting situation.

In 'Winning a Final' the athlete needs to separate himself from the past build-up of reaching the final. He needs to focus on the present (nowness), remain both physically and mentally relaxed, and develop a suitable tactical plan of action for the actual final match. The athlete should also be aware of the stress build-up to the final (refer to the section on stress and relaxation in Chapter 5). Proper utilisation of psychic and physical energy is of vital importance.

The final distinction of 'Consistently Making/Winning Finals' suggests that a culture of peak performance in pressure situations is evident. Northern Transvaal in rugby, Natal in hockey, Bruce Fordyce in the Comrades Marathon, Brian Mitchell in boxing, have all entered this final level. To consistently make finals, implies that all the factors involved in 'reaching the final' applies to this level: dedicated hard work; no easy methods; perseverence and discipline. 'When the going gets tough, the tough get going' is at the core of mind. Further, these teams or athletes have developed a culture of professionalism over time. Peak performance has become part of the team's ethos. Their psychology of winning is in fact their psychology of being. They trust themselves in pressure situations. They are in touch with their activity. They know themselves during action. In a sense, they have found enlightenment during their journeying.

In working with the Natal rugby team before the 1992 Currie Cup final against Transvaal, we developed the theme that 'striving for quality in action (in whatever is done), is at the core of a culture of excellence'. In our discussion, I commented that the team could make a quantum leap into the highest level of excellence. However, this would only be possible if the players were aware of the inner commitment and courage that was necessary.

The Natal players had to recognise that they had an opportunity to move onto the third level. In the process, a culture of excellence in their own play would emerge. Natal rugby as a whole could also make this quantum leap. There are no easy, short-cut ways to create this culture. Once this level has been reached, there are external expectations from the administrators, media and supporters that success will always occur. Nothing could be further from the truth. A culture of excellence has at its core dedication and the striving for quality. While it is difficult to reach a certain level of excellence, it is far more mentally and physically demanding to ensure that the quality of excellence is maintained over time.

## THE PSYCHOLOGY OF BEING

There are no quick fixes. Beware of those who try and convince you of 'proven' methods to achieve success. Top sportsmen have realised that winning goes beyond technique. They have managed to develop their own unique style of the psychology of winning. In this book, I have outlined some of the mental ingredients that I believe will make up the psychology of winning. These ingredients need to be integrated into the self-concept. The mix and proportion, is self-determined. In other words, the athlete needs to feel inwardly comfortable in using those ideas that will fit for him. There is no set formula of what ingredients to use. The timing becomes important; timing is an element that many sportsmen and coaches ignore. Time implies change – What works today may not work tomorrow. Learning about self, during competition, is vital. The psychology of winning is the psychology of being.

Having stated that there are no wonder methods to the psychology of winning, I do feel that the athlete needs to consider the following ideas when developing his own meaningful psychology of winning. Success in sport could best be achieved through:

- Dedicated and disciplined effort in training and during competition. There are no short cuts. There are no easy ways to reach the top.
- Balance between having fun during performance and the intensity to achieve success.
- Understanding the contradictory nature of the mind during action. Mind in action has been explored in Chapter 1.
- Linking with the dynamic interactive flow of sporting interaction. The nature of energy flow, heightened stress, and the ability to remain relaxed and focused during activity, are key concepts to become aware of. Further, upward and downward spirals of performance need to be understood. Appropriate action in dealing with these types of flow will enhance the standard of performance. Energy can get trapped by restrictive thinking or be wasted and dissipated through inappropriate action. Chapters 3 and 4 will examine these ideas in detail.
- Integrating the core elements of the psychology of being. These elements provide the building blocks for creative performance. They cannot or should not be separated into isolated parts that only function at certain given times. Instead, these elements are ways of being that should be integrated naturally into a meaningful whole.

These are the elements that are at the core of the psychology of being:

- Awareness Levels
- Dynamic Balance
- Focus and Flow
- Quality in Action
- Relaxed Performance
- Trust, No Judgement
- Allow time for Doubts

The intention is now to examine these elements in greater detail.

## Awareness Levels

The psychology of being requires that the athlete is aware of himself in action. He is tuned into his own movements, and that of his opposition. With this, he is able to read feedback messages from his body and from the opponent during performance. He becomes flexible in his response to these messages. It is important that the athlete develops his awareness levels. In order to do this, he should remain in the moment as much as possible. Further, he can ask his mind to 'think about its thinking' and become aware of internal and external messages.

Become aware of how your mind is operating in a situation. Awareness is the first step in initiating any changes that you may wish to introduce into your training or into the way you interact and behave on the field during actual performance.

As an exercise; while talking to another person, get in touch with what you are actually feeling and thinking in the situation. Are you bored? Is your mind occupied with any other concern? Have you really looked at, and noticed the colour of the person's eyes? What are the colours of his clothes? It is important to train your mind to accommodate and incorporate as much information in the present situation that you are interacting in. In sporting interaction, the winner is invariably the person who has heightened awareness.

In highly interactive team sports such as rugby, hockey and soccer, it is important that a player is aware of the space that he is in, and who is around him (opponents and team mates). Before receiving the ball, players must have already assimilated this information. This awareness is the foundation of decision-making when eventually the player is in possession of the ball. The thinking gets done before getting the ball, while creative action is allowed to follow (operating with 'no mind' ) when moving with the ball. Spontaneous decisions are then made in accordance with the flow of the action.

Further, being aware of those (opponents and fellow team members) around you, also allows you more time when in possession of the ball. In highly pressured international matches, the main psychological elements are the amount of time in making decisions and then being able to carry out the action; as well as the amount of space that a player has in which to move before he is challenged. I believe that psychological pressure on a team is increased, if time in possession of the ball is reduced, and space is constricted quickly. Time and space reduction results in poor decision making when a player receives the ball.

Brian Mitchell was highly tuned into how his body felt during training sessions in the build-up to a World title fight. This awareness of body sensations came through hard, dedicated training sessions. 'You get to know your body when you train hard. I knew that I was well prepared physically. This helped to motivate me,' commented Brian. Being aware of how he felt physically, gave Brian an inner security.

During his fights, Brian was often aware of what his opponent's corner men were telling their fighter. 'If you are relaxed during a fight, you can listen to what is going on,' said Brian. He then used this information to nullify his opponent. Despite the roar of the crowd, Brian could always hear his wife and his corner. He was able to block out that what was distracting, and yet be highly tuned into those sounds that he found important for improved performance.

## Dynamic Balance

In the psychology of being, a dynamic balance exists between all factors operating in a situation. Proper arousal is balanced with an inner relaxedness. Pushing ahead is balanced with the option of stepping back. Downward spirals of performance are not deepened through a mismanagement of activity. Instead, the intuitive and receptive feelings of the athlete are utilised in order to introduce the necessary balance between Yang and Yin activity (to be discussed in Chapter 3). Winners do not feed into their own stress cycles. They understand the rhythm of upward and downward cycles of performance. In the psychology of winning, it is imperative to become aware of how you are dealing with the downward spirals. Too much practice and too much determination with too much effort may result in an over-extension, and hence loss of psychological balance. This may escalate the problem; remember that 'too much practice makes Jack a dull boy'.

During performance, mind and body also need to be in dynamic balance. Bruce Fordyce contends; 'As much as your mind is strong, your body must go with it. In ultra-marathon running, if you really have got a major physical problem, it does not matter how strong your mind is, your body will win.' Your body has its limits. Elite sportsmen are highly tuned into their bodily sensations. Athletes rely on their bodies to execute remarkable acts.

In Tai Chi (a Chinese martial art), for example, the body movements are executed slowly so that one can become aware of your body centre. During body movement, an inner balance of body is necessary. In addition, the slow execution of action ensures that you become highly tuned into the slight differences of sensation and feeling of the body as it moves. In the process, the body becomes 'grooved', and bodily awareness is enhanced.

Too much thinking and strategising will interfere with the energy flow in the body. Top sport activity often requires automatic spontaneous movement. Too much mind, and too much planning in a situation, can inadvertently restrict the natural flow in activity. From reports in the press, it appeared that Nick Bester may have become too intense and too thorough in his planning in his running of the 1992 Comrades. Being the previous year's winner, he may have overplanned in his training and in the actual running on the day. On finishing sixth, he commented that he forgot to drink enough. This is such a fundamental error to make. Bruce Fordyce provides the insight, 'I know what Nick was doing because it has happened to me. He was thinking so hard about the race, and his tactics, and what's going on around him and what the other runners are doing, that he forgot to drink. Not that he forgot to drink, but that he forgot to drink enough.' Try not to think too hard during performance. I always tell sportsmen that too much analysis leads to paralysis. Mind and body balance is one of the most fundamental elements for peak performance.

Jonty Rhodes believes that sport should not be too serious or too mundane. Instead, a dynamic balance between being able to relax and have fun, as well as being able to concentrate on the simple things during performance, are what is necessary.

## Focus and Flow

The mind of a winner must be able to focus on a goal, and once focused should flow naturally and harmoniously in the journey towards the destination. Focusing is linked to clearness of mind, direction of energy flow, and relaxed concentration. Focusing implies that the inner desire and drive of the athlete has a determined direction in which to move.

The focus should not be on winning. Remember that winning is an end product. Instead, ask yourself what activity during performance would give you the best opportunity of winning. Focus on this activity or goal. Focus on simple action. The simpler the better. This should be most pronounced during periods of downward flow, when things are not going as well as was expected. Keep a clear, calm focus on what you wish to achieve. Focus is like a target. Your mental energy is directed onto this target.

During the flow, mind is not thinking. Instead, there is mind-body harmony. A state of being exists. 'No mind' and oneness occurs. The activity flows without effort. Doing what comes naturally, without force, is the essence of the period of flow.

The dynamic balance of focus and flow implies that in the flow the athlete loses himself. Tennis players refer to this flow as playing 'in the zone'. As the flow becomes disrupted in the action, the athlete re-aligns his focus on a simple goal. He is not easily distracted. His mind is clear in its vision. Then the athlete re-connects himself to the process of activity. He again moves with the flow. During the flow, the athlete is unconsciously aware of the critical moments in the unfolding action. He is prepared for these moments. He remains focused in what he intends doing.

Bruce Fordyce commented that there were periods in a race where he is almost in a trance. Despite this, he has heightened awareness while running. Bruce could, for example, pick out his second (a helper who assists the athlete with drinks, information, massage, medication) amongst a couple of hundred spectators. In speaking to Bruce, it seems that he is never too intense about trying to win a race. During the Comrades, he allows himself the opportunity to relax during the first part of the race, and as the race nears the end, he becomes more and more focused on the technical and tactical aspects of the race.

Jimmy Cook stated that there may be periods in his innings where he consciously says to himself; 'The bowlers are bowling well. I need to tighten up. I need to survive. It's O.K. not to score runs.' Jimmy attributes his ability to focus on this as being one of the main reasons for his success as a batsman.

Focus and flow are in dynamic balance. They are connected. They should dance together during performance. Ice hockey is a physically demanding sport where there is little or no time to think while you are in action. The team consists of a goalkeeper and five players on the ice at one time. There are 15 other players sitting on the bench. Players are being constantly changed by the coach. A player tends to spend a minute on the ice, and three minutes on the bench. This continues throughout the match (a match consists of three periods of 20 minutes).

The action on the ice is fast and furious. Players must remain focused during all this activity. In the mental preparation with the South African squad, we developed a mental format in order to focus and flow. Since there is no time to think while playing, I developed the STOP, THINK, ACT programme for the players.

Immediately on coming off the ice, the player is in the STOP phase. Here the player had to breathe, relax, clear his mind, get in touch with his body sensations (to increase awareness). Further, there was to be no judgement. If he had made a mistake, he could not afford to waste his psychic energy on something that now existed in the past. He had no control over that past situation. During this STOP phase, it is vital that the player is able to recover physically and to relax. The focus in this STOP phase is on relaxation, and clearing of the mind. The time duration of this phase may be one to two minutes.

After the STOP phase, the player moves into the THINK phase. Here he must re-focus on his simple goal, assess the opponent who he is playing against, and listen to the coach. In the hurly-burly of international ice hockey, it is imperative that the players are open to new input from the coach at critical times. There is often a lot of activity and shouting on the bench. The player must be tuned into important information that is given by the coach. He needs to respond to this input very quickly.

Approximately three minutes have now passed since the player has come off the ice. The coach nows yells, 'Go!' and the player is in the ACT phase. Here the player flows on the ice. He trusts his body. There is intense concentration on trying to implement his simple goal. But he is relaxed. During the ACT phase, it is important to enjoy the moment.

After about one minute in the ACT phase, the player is again pulled off the ice. The process now repeats itself. He is back in the STOP phase.

While watching the gymnastics at the Barcelona Olympics, I was again reminded of the importance of relaxed focusedness during high level competition. There are six pieces of apparatus (in the case of men gymnasts) that are simultaneously being run in one stadium arena. The crowd has the opportunity to watch any one of the events and to switch attention from apparatus to apparatus. In other words, there is ongoing activity around each of the pieces of apparatus.

By virtue of the nature of this contextual arrangement, one gymnast may be preparing to start his apparatus and may just be in the process of mounting the apparatus, when there is a sudden eruption of crowd applause (due to the completion of a routine on another piece of apparatus).

Being able to remain focused, despite the possible unpredictable distraction from the crowd, is a mental skill that is needed to ensure a high level of performance. The gymnast must be able to operate as if in a cocoon. Relaxed focusedness ensures that external distractions are blocked out.

### Quality in Action

The psychology of being has at its core the quest for quality of performance, improving the complexity of action without losing the simplicity in the execution. Quality is synonomous with inner pride and linked to professionalism in training, attitude to self and respect for the opposition. Quality ensures that the ego remains humble while winning. An inner balance allows true quality to surface; the ups and downs are handled with dignity.

The past exists in our memories, while the future exists only in our plans. True quality of action comes about when you are able to give all of yourself in the present. Pirsig (1974: 247) states that 'quality is the parent, the source of all subjects and objects'. What he means is that all purposeful action needs to emerge from a sense of becoming one with the moment that you are involved in. All your energies are focused. Quality of action will result if you are able to fully give everything of yourself, without trying to intellectualise or impress. Although quality cannot be fully defined, it is easily noticed. It is admired. It is respected.

In interaction with Brian Mitchell, I got this sense of quality. For every fight, Brian always felt that he wanted to be the best. In order to be the best, he always tried his best. This was only possible if his training programme left nothing to chance. Being well prepared allowed him to become the best. 'Sitting alone in my hotel room in a hostile country in the build-up to a world championship fight, was mentally tough. I kept on reminding myself what effort I had put into my preparation – all the blood, sweat and tears,' commented Brian. He had sacrificed tremendously. But this was necessary if he wished to achieve the quality of performance that would ensure success in the ring.

Quality goes beyond any action. Quality should be the source of all action. When kicking, running, training or communicating, quality is that which comes from a deep inner source. It is that which drives one for excellence. Top performers are constantly striving for perfection. As stated previously, the core of this striving is an inner enjoyment and fulfillment.

### Relaxed Performance

True winners are not obsessed with winning. Expectations of winning interfere with relaxed energy flow. Participation in any sport, at any level, must be activated by fun and enjoyment. Jonty Rhodes commented, 'If you are not enjoying yourself, it is pointless doing it. Not even winning is worth not enjoying yourself.' 'Enjoy the moment' is a phrase that I often use. Relaxed performance increases awareness, and allows for ease of flow during action.

Movements are smooth. In a sense, mind stands still, while body has fun.

Challenges should not cause a tightening of body and mind. Instead, the winner is able to become excited by any challenge. In the psychology of winning, it is necessary to test yourself. Obstacles need to be overcome. This is the nature of winning. The way these obstacles are dealt with, gives one more insight into the winner, than the actual end result of a winning score. Remaining calm under pressure is the hallmark of a winner.

Jimmy Cook keeps on reminding himself to keep calm while facing the world's fastest bowlers. As an opening batsman, Jimmy states that this calmness allows him to wait for the ball travelling at speeds in excess of 140 k.p.h. 'You do not want to be rushed and tight, while playing your shot,' says Jimmy.

Bruce Fordyce says that an ultra-marathon runner must never panic. In my discussion with Bruce, I asked him whether a runner's mental panic can feed into his body, causing him to tighten up, which in turn may activate cramping. He believed that this may be possible, and then commented on my question from the body's perspective: 'Sometimes in Comrades I have had little cramps that start, and then you say to yourself; "O.K. don't panic, you know what to do here, just change your stride a little." You can play around a little with your stride, or slow down a bit.' Bruce did feel that if there was something major wrong with your body, it did not matter how mentally tough you were, it would be impossible to keep on running. What is interesting to me is how his mind responds to sensations in the body during performance. Bruce is so tuned into his body that he knows what each ache or pain means. Further, he seems to know how to respond to these bodily messages.

Boxing is often a ruthless sport where pumped up aggression is evident. In discussion with Brian Mitchell, I posed the question of whether relaxation was important for fighters in the ring. 'If you cannot relax, you cannot think. It is important to relax under pressure. This is what makes a good fighter,' he remarked. He then outlined the main difference between professional boxing and street fighting. 'In the ring it is often live or die. Yet, if your opponent hits you, you cannot get angry and cross. You take your time and you want to think about how to respond. In the ring it is all about controlled aggression, and this depends on whether you are relaxed or not.'

## *Trust, No Judgement*

Value judgements create unnecessary distinctions in mind, that then influence the perceptions and restrict the action. Creative expression of energy flow will be hindered by judgements of behaviour. The true winner does not need external reinforcements and judgements from authority figures. He also does not actively seek approval through the results that he may have obtained. Instead, the psychology of being implies an egoless detachment from all that is achieved. Performance is not judged during performance.

Quiet contemplative inner reflection is necessary after performance however. Clear plans are outlined in mind. A new focus for action is created. While in meditation, the athlete 'stands still' in order to move forward. The dynamic balance between stillness and action is nurtured. During difficult periods, the athlete needs to become one with his sporting koan. It is during these periods that he comes to learn most about his inner soul. He needs to enter the heart of his sporting problem without judgement.

What is needed is that the mind should trust the body to perform, without trying to control the process. Trusting the process means that the winner knows he has fully prepared mentally and physically, and therefore looks forward to the unfolding journey. He understands that new learning will take place. He trusts himself in these situations.

In team sports, the true winner trusts his team members implicitly. He never allows his focus to stray onto the negatives of fellow players. He trusts that they will be able to resolve their own difficulties.

On a deeper level, the athlete trusts that whatever happens on the field, has occurred in order to test his inner strength. He does not seek easy ways out of the situation. Instead, he trusts that he has the necessary mental and physical ability to allow himself the opportunity to confront the difficulty.

## Allow Time for Doubts

The psychology of being implies a humanness. Doubts that may surface in your mind in the build-up to competition are normal. These are important messages that your unconscious may be wanting to give you. Take time to listen to these concerns. Do not try and exclude them because you feel that they are not positive. If you do ignore these concerns, they are likely to surface in those situations in which you would not want them to occur. Doubts are your mind's form of protection. Be gentle and patient with these thoughts. Once acknowledged, a more meaningful psychological balance is attained. The true winner acknowledges his humanness. He is not a mechanical machine.

Bruce Fordyce believes that part of his success in running the Comrades marathon is that he is very cautious and scared at the start of the race. 'I hope that I will just finish feeling all right. It is a long, tough struggle. I always hope that it will be a good race. I never think of winning, just doing well. As the race progresses, I get more and more confident.'

## BEYOND WINNING

The psychology of mind is not a game. Therefore mental preparation should never be evaluated in terms of a sporting result. The coach should try to avoid talking 'winning'. All sportsmen play to win. This is a given. All sportsmen should be committed in their efforts to succeed. As soon as you start talking 'winning', you are creating a reality that implies that losing reflects mental weakness and failure.

The psychology of being is at the core of the psychology of winning. The true winner is one who realises that there is no end to the journey. There may be resting points. Therefore, as coach, it is important to focus on the journey during sporting action. On a sports field, tasks need to be completed, roles fulfilled, and simple goals achieved during the journey. This will ensure the greatest possiblity for a favourable end result.

The psychology of being goes beyond winning. It becomes a way of functioning. The elements in the psychology of being are not techniques. Instead, they are the building blocks for exciting involvement with the inner self and others (opposition or fellow team members), during sporting interaction.

Everyone is seeking for the magic formula of winning. The more one seeks, the less one finds. We are continually seeking. The psychology of winning emerges after the intensive rush and desire to achieve has stopped. Once the dust has settled, the picture becomes so much clearer.

## CHAPTER 3

# Energy flow, pattern and quantum leaps

It is the intention in this chapter to explore the interactive flow of sporting activity. I believe that athletes and coaches need to become aware of the pattern of energy flow during a match. Although pattern and flow are not easily defined, these terms reflect movement of activity over time.

As sporting activity unfolds, natural ups and downs over time occur. You will have matches where everything just happens. During other matches nothing goes right. Remember that all activity moves in pattern and cycle. This is a fundamental law of nature.

When team meets team in sporting interaction, a pattern of activity emerges. The flow of activity during a match is complex. Some teams have good first-halves, then tend to fade in the second half. The opposite may be true for other teams, who start off slowly and then improve as time goes on. These patterns may continue in time.

There are critical moments in the match that can change the pattern of flow. Natural stoppages during highly interactive team sports, like scoring a goal, injury, player substitution, half-time, are punctuations that alter the flow pattern. When two teams are playing against each other, pressure is being applied on the opposing team. Under stress, players tend to make mistakes. These errors feed into the flow pattern. Downward flow may be deepened. More stress is exerted. A goal may be the outcome. Or, the team may be able to weather the storm. In other words, the team which was dominating may not have utilised their opportunities. The see-saw now starts to change. And so on, over time.

Energy is the vital commodity of sporting performance. Without energy nothing can be achieved. Peak performances occur when the athlete is able to unleash 'chunks' of energy in a directed focused way. In team sports, synchronised energy results when each player is psychologically committed to the group and achieves his own specific simple goal. These individual goals are then connected to the group objective.


## TAOISM

I believe that the ideas and philosophy of Taoism provide exciting insights into the nature of performance in sport. The ancient Chinese classic, the *Tao Te Ching* contains the principles of Taoism. Taoism primarily takes nature as its study, and looks at cycles of movement in time.

### Striving for Balance

Ancient Chinese thought believes that the universe is a vast Oneness. In this oneness, there is an interdependence and unity of all that exists. In other words, everything is dependent upon everything else, and this interdependent harmony is the basic principle of existence. This Oneness of existence is called *Tao*.

Integration of opposing forces into a harmonious whole is a fundamental principle of Taoism. 'Harmony as a word has gentle overtones, but it is worth emphasising at this point that the process of achieving harmony is not necessarily gentle.' (Page, 1989:13)

Maintaining a dynamic balance between opposing forces needs to be incorporated into any activity. Be careful of not increasing your own downward cycle through activity that goes against the grain. Taking a step back to look will help provide a clearer picture of the situation you are dealing with. Do not stubbornly push forward, without understanding what the consequences of such action will be, otherwise, you may become unbalanced.

Of particular interest to sport is understanding the natural harmony and balance between mind and body; and the way the mind can over-extend itself in the quest for success. Problems that emerge on the sports field are invariably due to an imbalance on one or other level. It is therefore important that an athlete develops a balanced outlook regarding himself and his performance.

The belief that balance is vital for healthy living is at the core of Taoism. For example, balanced diet: 'You are what you eat'; stress management approaches that emphasise a balance between play and hard work; the balance between physical exercise and work at the office; a balance between materialism and spiritualism. Opposites need to be integrated into a whole. The present movement in health care is driven by this fundamental understanding of dynamic balance.

'Health in human ecosystems refers to a vital balance of diverse forms of experience and behaviour...to engage in an effort of maximisation or minimisation, rather than diversity, leads to the escalating sameness defined as pathology.' (Keeney, 1983:126)

### Utilising Natural Power

The Tao Te Ching offers wisdom as to the ways in which human beings may bring themselves into harmony with cosmic power. Cosmic energy is contained in the Oneness. We need to become connected to the Oneness in order to utilise the energy.

'The Tao is a path of reflection and co-operation. The Tao teaches that all life is process. We and our world are continuously evolving. As we follow our path into the future, we can move from turmoil and imbalance to restore our oneness with nature and one another.' (Dreher, 1990: xv)

The life blood of the Tao is *Chi*. Chi is generally translated as being 'vital energy'. It encompasses, besides other energies, psychic and unconscious energy.

In the process of moving, the vital energy divides into *Yin* and *Yang* Chi. The Yin Chi, or energy of the feminine principle, is non-aggressive, yielding, quiet, intuitive, co-operative and receptive. The Yang Chi or energy of the masculine principle, is strong, aggressive, active, dynamic, direct, competitive and outgoing. The Yin and Yang flow together to form objects. Everything is composed of a combination of Yin and Yang Chi. Natural harmony and balance are strived for in the dynamic interaction of Yang and Yin Chi.

Life is composed of interacting complementary opposites. The interaction of Yang and Yin Chi creates pattern. It is also important to understand that the flow is cyclical. When Yang attains fullness, Yin is momentarily empty, only for Yang to recede and Yin to emerge. In the *I Ching* (Chinese book of changes), various life situations emerge and are formed due to the Yin and Yang interaction. I Ching also offers wisdom of how one could deal with the situation that is being confronted (see Cleary (1986); Baynes and Boardman (1984) for further information about I Ching).

It is now necessary to examine the interplay between Yin and Yang energy as they manifest in competitive sport.

Competitive sport is primarily Yang orientated. Aggressive expression of energy during sports performance, and the striving for success are Yang expressions. Pushing ahead and extending oneself to the limit is evident in sporting contexts. Assertiveness and confidence are always sought after by athletes.

Coaches expect teams and athletes always to be highly motivated, in order to perform better and better. The obsessive desire to win at all costs creates excessiveness in one direction without understanding that this creates a lack in another area. Overextension occurs. In the process, athletes may become unbalanced and unable to absorb themselves in the process of sporting interaction, without an obsessive concern about results and success.

Expectations of higher and higher achievement can result in a loss of motivation and a feeling of apathy. In a sense, this is actually the opposite of what is intended. The intense desire to succeed and achieve may become psychologically and physically draining. In the May 1992, *Junior Sport Magazine* I recommended to young athletes to get in touch with those elements in the sport they play, that excites them. This is the deep inner drive that should be nurtured. This inner source should thrill you.

In the mental preparation of the Natal rugby team for the 1990 Currie Cup rugby final, I introduced Yin elements such as relaxation and breathing as a way to develop an inner balance. The players responded positively. By allowing time to rest and be still, they were providing opportunity for the regeneration of assertive Yang Chi. 'Keep empty and you will be filled'.

## *Yield, if Necessary*

The yielding intuitive Yin Chi has been cut off by most competitive sportsmen. This is most pronounced when the athlete is not achieving the goals or standards of performance that he or the coach have set. One feels 'the wall'. Nothing seems to be working. There is invisible resistance. There is no ease of flow. These feelings need to be listened to. They are giving you an important message about yourself and the situation that you find yourself in. You are either not moving in the correct direction, or you are not responding in a suitable way, or the timing is wrong for the action you are trying to implement.

Brian Mitchell kept a training diary of all his physical workouts leading up to his fights. In addition, he made comments about how he felt physically, mentally and emotionally. With this information about himself, Brian intuitively knew how far to push himself or when he needed to take things a bit easy. 'If I have 3/4 rounds of sparring, and I feel that I haven't got it, I just won't spar the next day. I might take a break, forget about my weight, go home, have a nice pasta. If I feel weak, I take it easy.'

In a sense, Brian was incorporating more Yin type of activities when he felt a bit off during training. He took a step back from the activity. Or he introduced some slight changes in his training programme. In this way he was able to maintain an inner balance. He nurtured himself when feeling physically or emotionally down. Despite this, Brian always knew that he would be both physically and mentally ready when the big fight arrived. He trusted himself. He had also learnt to trust his training programme.

## *Be Gentle*

Water is a symbol for the power of Tao. It flows naturally, conforms to its environment, yet possesses tremendous strength.

> 'Nothing on earth
> Is more gentle and yielding than water
> Yet nothing is stronger.
> When it confronts a wall of stone
> Gentleness overcomes hardness;
> The power of water prevails.' (Dreher, 1990:217, Verse 78)

Elite sportsmen and coaches need to learn that pushing ahead in a competitive way, may unknowingly be the cause of more difficulty. Balance between firmness and gentleness needs to occur, without force. Intuitive hunches should be attended to. The harnessing of cosmic power in accordance with the principles of Tao, requires understanding of how one strives for inner balance, and the utilisation of Yin and Yang Chi.

I walked into the change-room of a soccer team which had lost its third consecutive match. The coach was expressing his anger and frustration. He was demanding more effort and commitment. The players seemed psychologically broken. Their body language reflected depression and despair. After the major confrontation by the coach, I had a deep sense that this team needed gentleness in order to improve. I also felt that the coach needed support and encouragement for his efforts and involvement. His outburst was a natural response. I asked the team and coach whether they thought things could get any worse. The unanimous response was 'Definitely not.' 'Good,' I said, 'so let's go and have a beer together. Tomorrow will bring better things.' Teams often need gentle handling in crisis situations. Relieving pressure is a fundamental part of achieving success.

### Tai Chi

Tai Chi, a Chinese martial art, is practised in order to attain harmony with the Tao. Tai Chi becomes a method of advancing one's spiritual development. The main principles of Tai Chi are (Galante, 1981:39):

Relaxation
Emptiness and Fullness
Slowness and Evenness
Balance
Coordination and Centering
Breathing
Concentration

These elements are connected. During my own Tai Chi practice, I initially found it extremely difficult to breathe in a slow, even rhythm as was being directed by the sensei during the execution of some basic exercises. In discussion with my sensei, he commented that relaxation and breathing feed into each other. Not being able to breathe in a deep slow rhythm is due to an inner tension. Yet, if one consciously tries to dictate the rhythm of the breathing, one forces the flow. This in turn will result in further tightening, which will further restrict your breathing. A vicious circle is unleashed. The main ingredients for creative performance and ease of flow in any activity are relaxedness, breathing, and physical and psychological balance.

Tai Chi movements are executed at an extremely slow pace. The idea is to allow the body to become aware of itself, as it is being grooved in certain action. Further, one is able to experience the unsteadiness in movement, as new learning takes place. Feeling physically unbalanced is heightened during the slowness. This invariably results in an inner tension.

The slowness of action requires an inner focus of quiet concentration. This relaxed focusedness helps reduce the inner tension, which in turn allows the body to flow more naturally. In addition, relaxed, deep, even breathing is necessary for the execution of the movements.

Tai Chi movement strives for mind-body integration. Experiencing the intense interaction between mind and body during the execution of slow action, becomes the vehicle for achieving inner wholeness. This process may not make sense while you are reading. Instead, it needs to be experienced. The body movement provides the learning.

Tai Chi is a 'soft' martial art. It therefore incorporates more Yin-like elements in the training. It provides the opportunity for quietness and a time to experience the dynamic interplay of opposing forces. The phenomenon of 'full' and 'empty', for example, becomes evident while transferring weight from one foot to another in a slow even way. Some tasks require all the weight to be placed on one foot (fullness), while the other foot remains free (emptiness).

Achievement and success takes on new meaning in Tai Chi. It is a non-competitive martial art. The striving for success, therefore, is located within a person; and not between people. Win/lose does not exist in Tai Chi. This is an unnecessary distinction, that may fragment the oneness. Inner balance becomes the focus. When this is achieved, a new level is attained.

## NATURAL CYCLES — THE RHYTHM OF PERFORMANCE

'The wisest person
Trusts the process,
Without seeking to control,
Takes everything as it comes,
Lives not to achieve or possess,
But simply to be
All he or she can be.' (Dreher, 1990:66, Verse 2)

### Catch a Wave

As sporting interaction unfolds during a match, there will be ups and downs. Moments of relaxed performance are mixed with periods of stress during performance. It is important that an athlete is able to connect to the flow. It is like surfing; a number of waves flow and the surfer needs to decide which wave to take. The timing of this is crucial. Once on the wave, he is propelled by the wave's energy. During the ride, however, the surfer has to deal with certain 'breaks' or rips in the wave. He must be able to respond to these unique demands during his ride.

When an athlete becomes disconnected (in mind or body), during sporting interaction, his performance declines. It is like being out at sea, with a surfboard, and noticing and feeling that the waves come and go, yet not being able to catch a wave. Either the timing is not right, or you have not managed to get onto the board in the correct way so that you can ride the wave.

On a physical level, the flow is determined by how the players move the ball around in space. Who has possession of the ball? And for how long? And in what area of the field is the possession taking place? As this process moves on in time, players are moving around in space. Playing without the ball increases psychological stress. Frustration builds up. If a player cracks, then this moment can be utilised by the team applying the pressure.

I always tell players who are involved in interactive team sports like rugby, soccer, water polo and hockey that space and territory dictate the amount of pressure that can be applied. When in possession of the ball, team mates must try and create more space by intelligent movement off the ball. When you do not have the ball, close down the space as quickly as possible. This closure of the opposition's space needs to occur simultaneously by all players. If an individual alone tries to close down his opposite number, a one-two pass by the opposition players will result in his being beaten.

The time frame in which to view the energy flow, is an important factor. One could look at the pattern of a side during a match, and notice the highs and lows in the team's performance. Some teams, for example, are slow starters in a match. This may occur in most of the matches that are played in a season. Other teams may on the other hand, find their rhythm quickly, only to fade in the last 20 minutes of a match. If one then takes a number of matches over time, a further pattern emerges.

## Up, Up and Away — A Runaway!

There is an expectation and belief amongst athletes that performance increases exponentially over time as shown in Figure 2. In nature this represents a runaway, where there is no healthy balance. Phenomena that fit this graph are such things as population explosion, increase in AIDS, breakdown in the ozone layer, pollution increase, and growth in cancer cells. As you know, these are frightening problems that our society still needs to confront. So how come athletes still have this unrealistic expectation about performance?

The answer can be found somewhere in the deeper cultural beliefs of our technological society. Attaining more and more materialistic possessions is considered a reflection of success. It is worth mentioning that business executives constantly think of maximising profits, where each year, for example, sales personnel are given higher and higher targets to strive for. The bigger, better, higher,

further philosophy. I contend that these beliefs will be confronted
on a global level, as we move into the 21st century. Everything in
nature exists in dynamic balance. A new balance needs to be established in our wider society. Resources are limited. Resources need
to be carefully managed. The psychology of abundance needs to be
replaced by the psychology of connectedness and interdependence. As the change in thinking occurs, new perceptions of
wealth, success, and happiness will emerge.

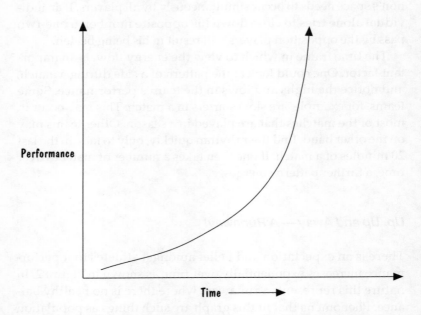

*Figure 2: Unrealistic 'mind' expectation of performance over time*

Athletes need to strive for perfection. Setting goals to achieve,
helps guide the direction of effort in training. Quality of performance should be at the core of every training session. Developing
an inner pride in the quality of your performance is necessary in
order to continue making progress in your field of endeavour. Yet
it is vitally important to capture and incorporate these qualities
into a healthy philosophy of the nature of sporting interaction.

## Be Ready, But Do Not Expect

I now attempt to present an understanding of the progress in performance, over time, that is more in line with nature. Think of yourself on a particular level (say club level). As you operate and practise on this level, you will notice that your performance moves in upward and downward flow. As you develop your competence at this level over time, you will start showing signs of 'quantum leaping' to the next level. Your performance should be consistent, coupled with an increase in your creativity. If your mind is now looking for reward and recognition to gain entry into the next level, you are seeking success and in the process you may start trying too hard. You will no longer operate in the present. Your performance will decline. This will prevent the leap into the higher level.

When your opportunity arrives (provincial selection), are you properly prepared to utilise the moment? There is no actual difference with regards to the demands. Most sportsmen perform best in their first season on a new level. They enjoy the challenge of testing their skills in a more demanding context. If you develop sufficiently within this level, you start preparing for the leap to the next level (international selection).

Again, consistency and increased creativity on this level will provide you with the opportunity to leap. Do not seek success.

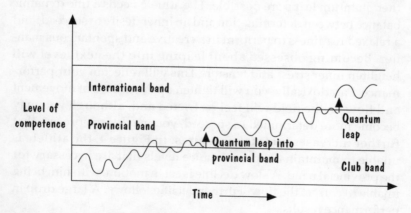

*Figure 3: Quantum leaps in overall performance over time*

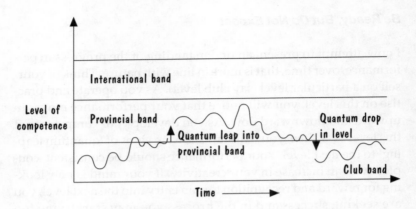

*Figure 4: Quantum leaps and drops in overall performance over time*

Instead, be fully prepared for the moment if an opportunity arrives. This has been extremely difficult for our South African athletes to deal with, due to our isolation in international sport. Remaining on the same level for too long creates rigidity in mind, as well as staleness in physical performance.

Figures 3 and 4 represent the rhythm of performance of two athletes over time. In Figure 3, the athlete is able to leap into the higher band. Depending on the athlete's capabilities within this level, further quantum leaps are possible. The athlete needs a fine dynamic balance between determination and an inner desire to succeed, and a relaxed readiness to perform in a creative and spontaneous manner. Becoming obsessed about leaping into the next level will heighten inner stress and tension. This will reflect in your performance. Paradoxically, you will tighten up. Your ease of movement and flow on the field will feel restricted and, although you may become more determined to succeed, you may start a process that further increases internal pressures. In Figure 4, the athlete is unable to maintain the performance levels that are necessary for the provincial band. A slow decline is set in motion, with him being unable to correct the flow. Further decline follows. A large drop in performance results.

## *Ride the Wave, Do Not Dig the Grave*

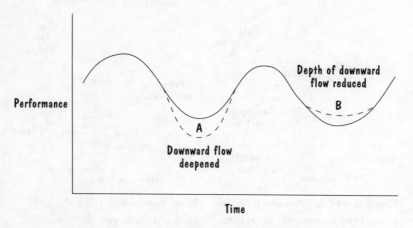

*Figure 5: Upward and downward flow of performance during a match*

Figure 5 outlines a flow pattern during a match. In situation A, the athlete deepens his trough. It is during the downward flow that the mind starts interfering in the process. A downward spiral is like quicksand. The more you struggle, the deeper you sink. In situation B, the athlete has managed to move out of the downward trend quicker and in the process lessens the depth of the trough. During a downward period, focus on your breathing. Listen to your own rhythm. This allows you to detach yourself from trying too hard. Further, it provides you with an opportunity to relax and release tension. Tightness is reduced. You may wish to hum a song during this period as another way to detach yourself from trying too hard.

During the upward flows it is important for the athlete to utilise the movement to his advantage. Top sportsmen who are tuned in to this period trust themselves and literally ride the wave. In cricket, for example, a batsman may have a run of innings where nothing goes wrong. Runs are scored with ease, and often he has luck in being dropped when he offers a chance.

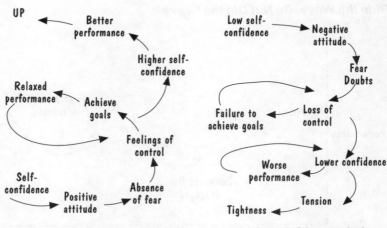

Move with the flow. Allow energy to direct    Do not push forward. Take a step back.
action. Enjoy the movement. No analysis.       Focus on a simple goal. Relive past
Optimise this period fully. Be humble.         success. Do not force. Be gentle with self.

*Figure 6: Upward and downward spirals*

In competitive sport, an athlete may become inwardly unbalanced in the downward spiral due to increased psychic and physical activity in the Yang mode (trying too hard, becoming more determined). Instead, the dynamic balance between mind and body can be achieved if Yin-like activity is also introduced.

### Critical Moments

In sport, athletes need to deal with both upward and downward spirals of performance. During the actual match, the flow moves upward and downward. There are critical moments in the flow. Changes in level of performance occur. It is vital that the athlete becomes highly sensitive to these moments. Upward spirals can be transformed into a downward trend. It is also during these periods that stress increases or is released.

Brian Mitchell stated that you live and die many times in a fight. This captures the essence of upward and downward flow during performance. Brian commented that there were some rounds where he thought that he would not be able to finish the fight only to feel renewed and energised a round or two later. Brian then expanded on the critical moments during a fight: 'You can feel it. You can see it in a guy's eyes and the way he moves. Your corner men may say to you, "you had him in trouble so why did you not open up", but they do not realise that you can see a bit more than them because you are closely involved in the situation.'

Knowing when to take that critical moment in boxing is the difference between a knock-out punch or being knocked out yourself. Brian explains, 'Your opponent may only be slightly hurt, and may be looking for a bit of time. And he is looking for wind, but he is not gone. He will be back for more. So you do not want to throw yourself out by throwing big bombs.' 'What could happen?' I enquired. 'Well you can get knocked out yourself or you could tire yourself out, and the next thing you realise is that he is coming at you,' stated Brian. To recognise critical moments in a fight is vitally important. However, what to do in these moments will determine the eventual outcome of the fight. There may be moments during a fight where the correct decision may be not to push forward and throw punches; even though it may appear to others that that critical knock-out moment has arrived.

In cricket, there are periods in the play where the batsmen are on top, being able to score runs freely and comfortably. At a fall of a wicket, the ease of scoring runs immediately stops as the bowlers apply pressure on the batsmen. Jimmy Cook consciously reminds himself before going out to bat, that there might be periods in his innings when the bowlers will be bowling well. 'In these periods, I say to myself that I must hang in there. I must stay alive, rather than to try and hit them out of this attack right now. I become mentally strong, with increased concentration. I also tighten up my game to minimise mistakes. The time will come when they will break. They will send a few loose deliveries or there may be a bowling change.' It is significant that Jimmy becomes aware when the bowlers are on an upward flow cycle. He states that bowlers are allowed to bowl well. Jimmy further contends that he must be patient during this period. 'Just one bad ball can change the flow. You must be prepared to wait for this ball.'

In playing against Transvaal in the 1992 Currie Cup final, the Natal players knew that the last 20 minutes of the match would be a 'critical period'. Transvaal were a physically fit and well tuned team, that were always able to exert tremendous pressure on the opponents in this period. It was during this period, that the Natal players had to maintain their focus on the game plan, as well as, to concentrate on their own individual tasks. The match was going to be won or lost in that critical last 20 minute period.

### The Two Rugby Test Matches

South Africa could not have wished for a more difficult re-entry into the international rugby arena. Without any match preparation, the team tackled the two top nations, New Zealand and Australia, within a week in August 1992. This would have been a most daunting task for any team that had been familiar with and accustomed to the demands of test match rugby. It was now expected of the rusty South African team to peak twice, both mentally and physically, within a week. In addition, the expectations of the media and the public were high. One supporter's banner read 'You are not the world champions until you beat the Springboks'.

We were beaten convincingly in both matches, in all facets of play. Having said this, I feel that our players did remarkably well. They showed courage and commitment on the field, despite the lack of experience. In the first test match against the All Blacks, the South African team absorbed tremendous pressure in the whole of the first half. This was to be expected as the team was coming to terms with the demands of test match rugby. At half-time, the score was 10–3 to the All Blacks. In watching the match, I felt that our team had managed to maintain its focus, despite the intense pressure of mostly having to defend and tackle. Defensively, we had coped well.

The half-time break is a natural punctuation in the flow. The next ten minutes would give an indication of the effects of the first half pressure. The South African players seemed well motivated as a team at the start of the test. This had carried them through the first half. Now in the second half, the players had to maintain their own individual focus, as well as unleash the necessary energy for high activity.

Within the first 20 minutes of the second half, the All Blacks had utilised an upward flow cycle that extended their lead to 27-10. With five minutes left to play, there was a marked change in activity flow. The All Blacks went into a deep downward trough, and in the process lost concentration, while the South African players found a rhythm and became highly energised. It was a phase in the match where the South African players were relaxed in their efforts (they were so far behind that they threw the ball around and in the process stretched the All Blacks). Coupled with this, there was a marked drop of physical energy from the All Blacks (probably due to the effects of playing at high altitude, as well as having relaxed psychologically due to the score at that stage). Nevertheless, in the space of five minutes, the South African team had scored two tries, both being converted. The final score was 27–24 to the All Blacks.

A test match is often won or lost in a space of a couple of minutes. There are critical time periods where teams may lose focus. The build up of pressure can fragment the cohesiveness of a team. Being able to utilise the upward flow cycle and exert pressure on the opposition, results in mistakes being made by the opponents. If this is converted into scoring points, then the upward flow has been well utilised.

The after-match television comments of the two captains were interesting. The captain of the South African team, Naas Botha, felt that the South Africans were not beaten by the All Blacks, but instead had lost the match themselves. There were also complaints about the attitude of the Australian referee, Mr Sandy MacNeill, towards the South African players, . The captain of the All Blacks, Sean Fitzpatrick, felt that his players had lost concentration in the last ten minutes, as their minds had drifted off in wanting to get back home. The players had been away from home for eight weeks (the side had arrived in South Africa after completing a six-week tour of Australia, in which they had played three tests). These different perspectives on how the last few points were won, exemplify the multiple experiences and realities of a match.

From the press reports of the match, as well as the comments of Naas Botha, it appeared as if we had not renounced our perceived world crown. After the All Blacks test, our expectations of success were still very high. These expectations can inadvertently create more pressure on the players. In thinking about the team, I wondered whether the players would be able to recover quickly enough from both the physical and mental drain of that test, and be ready for the Australians in a week. I wondered whether we were expecting too much, too quickly.

The test against Australia was played in terribly muddy conditions, where the ground underfoot was slippery. Again, the South Africans played with a motivated tenacity in the first half, doing excellent defensive work. At half-time the score was 8–3 to the Australians.

As the second half progressed, the Australians exerted more and more pressure. With 11 minutes left to play, the score was still 8–3. However, in the closing 11-minute period, the Australians had extended their winning margin to 26–3. Eighteen points were scored. But how should we interpret this sudden downward spiral in performance?

The total collapse in the team in the last 11 minutes of the match needs to be put in perspective. The first point that I wish to make is on the regeneration of physical and mental energy. The players were not physically and mentally accustomed to the demands of playing test match rugby. There is no need to feel ashamed about this. The only problem was that the task was made even more difficult for the players by the intensity of playing two test matches within a week. The total disintegration in those last 11 minutes was due to the accumulated pressure of 160 minutes of test match rugby (two consecutive tests in a week), with no period of relaxed unwinding.

On the Wednesday after the All Blacks test, the players were again in intensive training to try and peak for the Australian match. The South African players had to put the All Black test behind them quickly and re-direct their focus on the Australian match. Within a week, the South African team were expected to deal with two different styles of opposition play. This is a form of culture shock for any team, never mind the South African team who had been isolated for so long.

From an Australian perspective, they had played three test matches against New Zealand in Australia. The side was hardened to the demands of test match rugby. Further, it was a team that had played together since 1989, culminating in their winning the World Cup in England. After a week's rest at home, they embarked on a two week tour to South Africa. The three matches in the build-up to the test were used to help peak the team for that single test. The side had only that one test to focus on. The natural energy reserves in this team far outweighed those in the South African team due to the build-up to the test. This made the Australians most dangerous in the latter stages of the match.

While tactically the South African team may not have been equipped with the latest ideas, the players did show the necessary commitment in facing the challenges of modern day rugby. After the defeat, the press contended that Dr Danie Craven had made suggestions of wanting to cancel the 1992 Currie Cup final, in order to build the South African team. The idea was to try and send the team on a tour to Argentina, before embarking on their seven-week tour of France and England. I believe that the process of developing a team takes time. Creating more demands in a rushed and intense manner, may in fact escalate the problem.

Our national coaches need the support to make long-term plans. South African rugby problems will not be eliminated overnight. Learning occurs best if there is a plan of action that has been developed through calm introspection and inner reflection. Our national players will need gentle guidance, as well.

The learning process needs to ensure that by the 1995 World Cup competition, the team has developed a creative synergy. The period between now and then may prove to be difficult and painful. This is sometimes necessary to ensure that learning takes place. We are presently at a critical point in the history of our rugby. The old assumptions in thinking need to be challenged; otherwise we may remain stagnant. This may be especially necessary in the administration of rugby matters. Invariably, it is at this level that the structures and contexts are created in which to operate. Administrators develop a way of thinking or culture that permeates down into the sport as a whole.

### Natural Breaks in Activity

There are natural punctuations in competition (half-time, having just scored, having won/lost a set, injury, the end of a round in boxing), that will affect the flow, transforming upward into downward flow or vice versa.

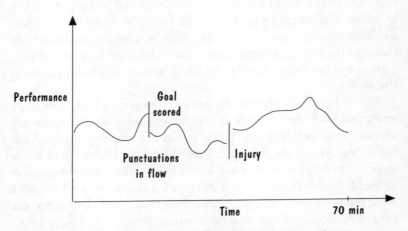

*Figure 7: Flow during a hockey match, with punctuations*

Jimmy Cook contends that lunch, tea and drink breaks are bad for batting. 'Bowlers always find it easier after these breaks. Maybe it is because they do not have to concentrate much. Invariably, a wicket always falls after a break even though you may have consciously said to yourself that you should tighten up. It is just readjusting. You go back into a change-room and there is different light, maybe it is darker. You come back out onto the field and you just haven't tuned into what you have been doing beforehand.'

In discussion with Jimmy, it became apparent that the batsman has to deal with a number of contextual changes: from facing the bowlers out on the field, and with it the quiet inner concentration, to entering a change-room where the batsman is able to relax, as well as interact with fellow team members; and then back onto the field having to quickly gather one's inner concentration again. The fielding side, on the other hand, are able to regroup during the break. Bowlers are able to rest and enjoy some refreshments; weary legs can also be massaged. After the break, the fielding side invariably takes the field feeling rejuvenated and energised.

### The Pattern that Emerges over Time

Max Planck, a quantum physicist, showed that energy is radiated in chunks or quanta, rather than a steady continuous flow over time. This energy is radiated through activity on the sports field in 'packages' and spurts.

There is always upward and downward flow in a match, as each team is releasing energy in chunks at different times. This energy flow interacts, sometimes with a nullifying effect. An upward burst of energy flow, coupled with a downward trend of energy from the opposition, may result in a form of dominance which may then lead to a goal being scored.

In interactive sports, a team develops its own wholeness and in the process transmits its own energy. When team meets team in competition, the combined wholeness of the two energy flows interact. A team that is able to maintain its own wholeness, and in the process fragment the links and connections in the other team, is most likely to move according to its own rhythm. In the process, the pattern of play that will emerge will be more in line and congruent with the team which is able to maintain its unity of energy flow.

A team develops its own personality over time. While watching Egypt play Germany in a hockey international during the Barcelona Olympics, I was struck by the way culture impacts on sport. It was interesting to see how two contrasting styles merged together in interaction.

The Egyptians were prone to emotional outbursts, which were directed at opposition players, the umpires and fellow players. The Egyptians were volatile, and at times became easily distracted. In comparison, the German team were disciplined and methodical in approach. No emotional expression was evident, as each player continued to fulfil his role on the field. Of interest to me was how these attributes interacted and fed into each other.

While emotional expression can distract opposition players into making mistakes, the Germans in fact became more clinical and task orientated as the Egyptian players gave vent to their feelings. This in turn, put more pressure on the Egyptian players, and in the process heightened their own emotionality. A circular pattern started to emerge. The more disciplined and methodical the Germans, the more disruptive and emotional the Egyptians. The final score was 8–2 to the Germans.

Giving vent to feelings on the field can release heightened frustration. I know of players who are able to refocus quickly after emotional expression, and in the process become more determined. The tennis player, John McEnroe, has such a personality. His outbursts invariably lift his own standard of play while impairing the concentration and focus of his opponent. This delay also breaks the flow of activity. On restarting the match, the nature of the rallies (or interactive flow) would have changed. The player who is able to recapture his focus quickest, will start dictating the play.

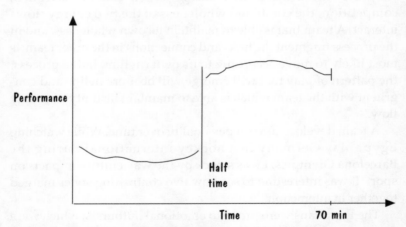

*Figure 8: Performance flow of a provincial hockey team*
*Below average slow first half, with high competence in second half*

Figure 8 reflects the pattern of energy flow of a provincial hockey team that emerged over a seven match period. They were slow starters and the first half proved difficult for them to get the necessary flow in their game. At half-time, a remarkable change always seemed to emerge. The team was able to lift their work rate. The speed of passing the ball increased. The cohesiveness between the players was readily evident through player communication on the field. During the unfolding interaction of play, tremendous pressure was exerted on the opponents. Invariably the opposition's play disintegrated, resulting in good wins for the team. From two opposing perspectives (the coach of the team and the coach of the opposition), this pattern of flow provides useful information.

For the coach of this team, this pattern needs to be understood if he wishes to improve the overall competency and performance of the team. This may be needed during an important final. But what are the factors that may be hindering the team from unleashing its creative activity and energy in the first half? In order to get this information it will be necessary for the coach to look at the pattern of interaction between the players (including his own interaction in the team).

A team is a living organism and therefore follows predictable patterns of dynamic interpersonal interaction. Certain patterns leading up to the match may need to change, if the coach wishes to change the flow of activity during the match. The team may need to arrive earlier at the field, or the nature of the warm-up period may need to be reviewed. The coach should also reflect on his own verbal input into the team before the start of the match. He may be talking too much, and in the process creating an overload. Alternatively, he may not be giving enough input to the team.

From the other perspective, the opposition coach should focus on how to counter this activity flow through his own team's strategy plan. In particular, will his team be able to exploit the slow activity of the opponents during the first half? How will he be able to generate sufficient synergy in his own team in the first half? How should he deal with the expected pressure in the second half? In this way, the coach can modify his own team's interactional pattern in order to create a more appropriate activity flow on the field, in order to provide the best possible chance for a favourable end result.

### Hockey at the 1992 Barcelona Olympics

While at the Barcelona Olympics, I mapped out the energy and performance patterns of four of the teams over a two-week period. The teams were Australia, Pakistan, Great Britain, and Egypt. Each team played seven internationals during the Olympics.

The pattern was mapped according to the time periods when the team performed best, as opposed to those periods when standards dropped. Further, periods in which goals were scored for, and goals scored against were noted. In addition, the energy levels and work rate of players were noted as the match progressed in order to add further complexity to the pattern that emerged.

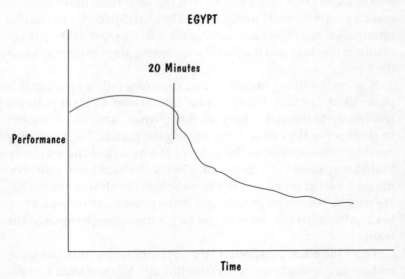

*Figure 9A: The pattern of performance flow of Egypt during the 1992 Olympic hockey*

During the first 20 minutes, the side was highly energetic. In this period, Egypt were able to disrupt the flow of the opposition. The team's best overall standard of performance occurred in this first 20 minute period. During the match with Australia, for example, the Egyptians scored in the first five minutes of the match.

Their pattern of play and the state of the team tended to disintegrate as the opposition settled into the match. The high performance dropped markedly after they had conceded a goal. The players lost their individual focus, and in the process became disruptive within the team. In addition, players had emotional outbursts towards umpiring decisions. The team's energy was turned inward and was destructive and negative.

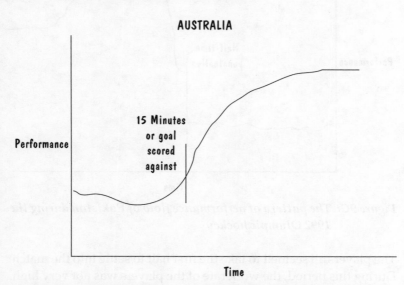

**AUSTRALIA**

*Figure 9B: The pattern of performance flow of Australia during the 1992 Olympic hockey*

The players seemed highly aroused. Basic errors in play were most evident in the first 15/20 minutes of a match. The side was most vulnerable during this period. Energy was expressed through frantic activity. The metaphor that came to mind, was that of an activated swarm of bees. The players seemed on a mission, with high motivation. Unfortunately, composure and the ability to remain relaxed on the ball suffered as a consequence.

Against Germany in the final, they conceded a goal in the second minute of the match. As time moved on in a match, the overall standard of performance improved. Players had to burn off hyped-up energy through high work rates. The side responded well to hardship and it seemed that they were able to relax easiest when coming from behind.

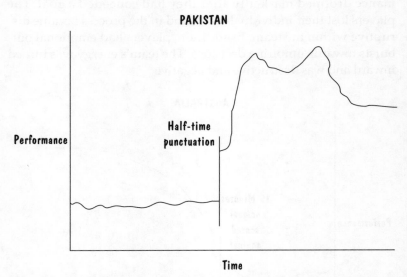

*Figure 9C: The pattern of performance flow of Pakistan during the 1992 Olympic hockey*

The players all seemed to take the first half to settle into the match. During this period, the work rate of the players was not very high. It appeared that the team needed time to develop its wholeness and synergy. In the initial periods of the match there was a great deal of individual play, without the necessary interdependent play.

A quantum leap in the team's performance seemed to occur after the half-time break. There were periods of exceptional creativity with an outstanding display of skill. Against the Commonwealth of Independent States, Pakistan scored four goals in a 20-minute period (final score 6–2). In a five-minute period after half-time the team scored two goals against Holland, after being 1–1 at the break. The final score in this pool match was 3–1. In the semi-final against Holland, Pakistan were 0–2 down at the half-time break. In a 25-minute period during the second half, Pakistan scored four goals (final score 4–3). Playing against Spain, the score was 1–1 into ten minutes of the second half. In 25 minutes of exhilarating interactive flowing hockey, Pakistan scored five goals (final score 6–1).

The players used the upward flow to full advantage. Individual flair was mixed with team unity. Players were enjoying themselves. Individual decision making was excellent and fitted into the interactive flow of the team. It also appeared as if time had slowed down for the players. The opposition seemed demoralised in the face of such creativity.

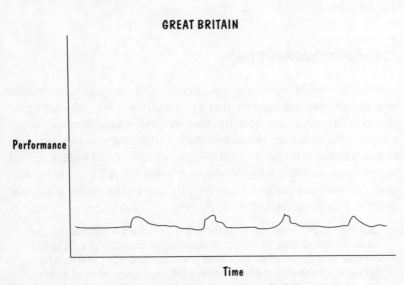

**GREAT BRITAIN**

Performance

Time

*Figure 9D: The pattern of performance flow of Great Britain during the 1992 Olympic hockey*

The team struggled to attain any great heights in the two-week period. The energy levels of the players were low. The team appeared to be flat and lethargic. During matches there were sporadic, yet short-lived, energy bursts that improved performance.

From discussion with some insiders, the team had not managed to resolve a number of interpersonal difficulties. It was not a happy team. Great Britain had won the gold medal at the 1988 Seoul Olympics. Older players who had won gold at the previous Olympics, and the younger more inexperienced group of players, needed to integrate. This may not have fully occurred. In the process, the team reduced its synergetic power. In addition, there were high expectations from supporters and the media. This may have further increased the stress on the team.

A team needs to be able to live with itself off the field. Valuable energy can be wasted on destructive processes within a team. Players need emotional support and security in a team. While on the field, this emotional support will increase the inner commitment of the individual to the team. Further, players can relax in performance when feeling secure.

## IDEAS PRODUCE ENERGY

One of the most interesting discoveries made in quantum physics was that an electron can be either a particle or a wave, depending on the experimental situation. In other words, an electron may show particle characteristics in one situation, and reveal wave-like aspects in another experimental situation. The observer and experimental apparatus determine how the electron will respond. However, electrons are neither fully particles nor fully waves, but rather a mixture of both. This is referred to as the particle/wave duality.

'Subatomic particles have no meaning as isolated entities but can be understood only as interconnections, or correlations, between various processes of observation and measurement. Particles are not seen as consisting of any basic 'stuff', but as bundles of energy. Energy is associated with activity, with processes, and this implies that the nature of subatomic particles is intrinsically dynamic.' (Capra, 1982:69)

Mind and thought operate according to the principles of quantum physics. Mind is actually a powerful generator of energy. Thought becomes the initiator and director of energy flow. Thought occurs at lightning speed (speed of light) and therefore can be seen to operate according to the principles of quantum physics. Quantum leaps in performance on sporting fields are therefore dependent on quantum leaps in thought and actual energy release in activity.

Your focus of energy release will be directed at the content of thought existing in your mind at a given time. In other words, your ideas become the director of energy flow. Continually thinking about an unresolved interpersonal issue in a team, for example, will use up vital energy, which could in fact have been utilised in a match.

## Ideas Reflected as Waves

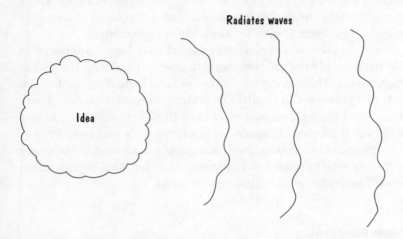

Radiates waves

Idea

*Figure 10:  Thought acts like a subatomic particle: the idea can be captured as a particle, yet also transmits waves over distance*

Figure 10 shows a thought as being an idea or concept that can be conveyed (its form or shape can be equated to that of a particle), while the manner of transfer (consciously or unconsciously) reveals a 'vibe' or wave-like flow. This wave-like flow can transcend space. The wave-flow operates on a conscious and unconscious level.

Important discoveries and ideas often seem to occur at the same time in locations that are thousands of kilometres apart. It would therefore not surprise me that somewhere on earth there are other individuals who are trying to formulate ideas in much the same way as I am attempting to do. Their ideas may be helping me to create meaning in my own mind, which in turn may help them to formulate their own ideas further, through the wave transfer of my thoughts. While this may seem strange to some people, I have come to understand that there are unexplainable phenomena that quantitative, analytical science cannot even begin to investigate. The intricacies and complexities of the interconnected fabric of life are sometimes beyond total understanding.

Another example relates to the times when I share a thought with my wife, only for her to state that she was presently thinking about that idea and was going to tell me about her thoughts. These thoughts are unrelated to the normal cues in a context that usually trigger a particular idea in the situation at a given time.

Further, there have been times when I have been thinking of an old friend, only for the telephone to ring with him on the line to speak to me. These occurrences do not have logical rational explanations. However, it is difficult to deny their occurrence. There does seem to be unconscious energy flow between people and events that transcends space. Of importance, is that conscious or unconscious connections between people disconnected in space will still result in some form of energy transfer. This energy transfer will help 'shape' the situation you are in.


### When People Interact

Each person has a different energy resonance. The pace of walking or talking is different. The manner of speech varies, as well as the activity of eye movement. Some people are big in stature, while others are more compact in physique. In any interaction between two or more people, energy is being released and transferred on a number of different levels. Each person has his own energy flow pattern.

If you are sitting alone in work or thought, the presence of another person in the space that you have consciously or unconsciously defined for yourself, will result in a change in energy flow. One cannot not influence. One cannot not communicate (Watzlawick, Beavin and Jackson, 1967:48). Even silence communicates meaning. Communication transmitted consciously or unconsciously, verbally or nonverbally utilises and transmits energy.

In interaction, two basic energy patterns emerge; namely symmetrical and complementary connections (Watzlawick, Beavin and Jackson, 1967:67).

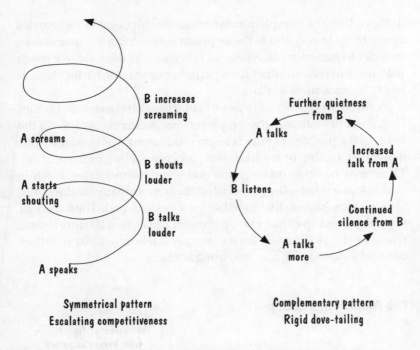

Symmetrical pattern
Escalating competitiveness

Complementary pattern
Rigid dove-tailing

*Figure 11: Interactional patterns between individuals A and B*

In the symmetrical relationship, there is a possibility of escalating sameness, whereas in the complementary connection, there is the possibility of rigidity of opposites.

An example of a complementary relationship in sport occurs when the coach tells the player to do something, the player becomes quiet and passively rejects the coach's input, which increases the coach's frustration and increases his talking to the player, which makes the player resentful and more quiet, and so on. An example of escalating symmetry is dirty play on the field, where player A fouls player B, who now goes all out to repay player A, and in the process kicks him, which causes player B to punch player A, and so on.

In these examples, spontaneous and creative energy can get trapped by the rigid circular pattern of interaction. The introduction of something different from one of the parties in the symmetrical relationship will ensure that a new level in the relationship is

achieved. In the complementary relationship, one of the parties
needs to try to respond in the opposite way during the interaction,
in order to generate a newness. In other words, the talkative coach
may need to remain silent for a period of time in order for the athlete to become more verbal.

A range of different types of relationships exist in a team.
Ongoing interactions between players are occurring on and off the
field. In the process, energy is being transferred. Some interactions
generate a feeling of togetherness, others a feeling of frustration.
There may be other interactions that leave one revitalised, while
others leave one feeling exhausted and emotionally drained. On
tour, players have to live together for weeks on end. The nature of
the relationships that exist between players will determine
whether the side generates a synergetic wholeness or whether
political subgrouping and infighting surfaces.

### *The Ripples in a Group*

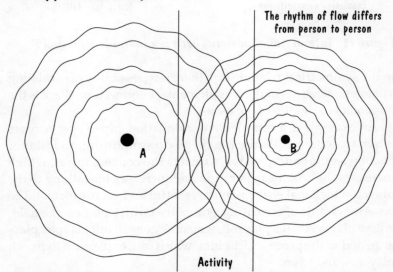

**Figure 12:  *Activity area of energy interaction between persons A
and B***
*Wave activity can either increase or decrease the connective
power*

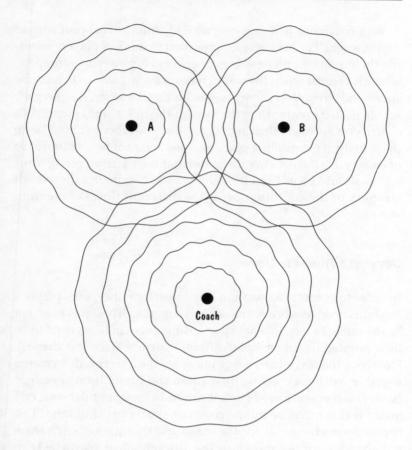

***Figure 13: The coach will affect the activity and energy flow***
*The coach needs to be aware of the impact of his intervention*

As a metaphor, take two stones of different size and shape. Now
throw them into a pool of water. Each stone will generate its own
waves flowing outwards. If these waves meet they either converge
to increase in size, or nullify each other in a disruptive manner with
splashes. In the process, other little spin-off waves and ripples are
created. The meeting place is a place of great activity. Notice that
each of the stones had produced a different size, speed and fre-
quency of ripple. At the meeting place, each of the independent ripples is transformed into a different flow in whatever form.

As a coach of a team playing a highly interactive sport such as rugby, football or hockey, it is important to think of players releasing their own ripples or waves of energy. A powerful synergetic whole is created when the waves meet in such a way as to increase speed and strength. Synergy is synchronised energy. A synergetic whole is also greater than the sum of the individual parts. As a coach, you are also releasing waves. But your focus should be on the activity at the meeting place. Become aware of how your waves of energy are influencing the activity at the meeting place. Your waves should be utilised in such a way as to enhance the overall strength of the combination of the different flows of meeting waves.

### Develop a Theme to Unite

In order to generate a quantum leap in performance, each player's thoughts need to work harmoniously together. Thoughts need not be the same. In fact, in team sports, differences in ideas need to be incorporated into the whole (different particle sizes and shapes). However, the wave-like energy release of the ideas needs to merge together, without creating disruption and dissipation of energy flow. This mergence needs to 'jell' around a meaningful theme, created for this purpose by the coach or sports psychologist. The theme forms the focus for the ideas and thoughts of each team member. Figure 14 shows how the different ideas (particles) can flow to a unifying theme (another particle), which in turn generates powerful wave flow and activity in action.

In discussion with the Natal rugby players before the 1990 Currie Cup final, a theme of 'We have an opportunity to make history' emerged. I asked the players to entertain this thought and as they did, a new meaningful reality was being created. This theme provided the necessary integration of the individual differences in the team. Differences in ideas were accepted and unified into a powerful whole. In the process, the potential for a quantum leap in performance was being forged.

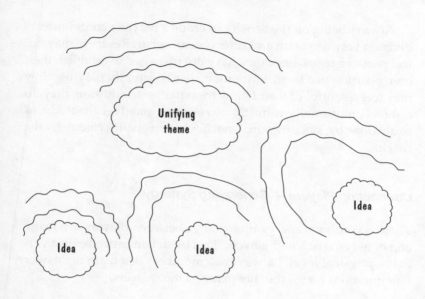

*Figure 14:  Waves of separate ideas need to merge into a unifying theme, which in turn generates energy for a possible quantum leap*

### Reserve Players

In team sports, I like to spend a lot of time with those players who are going to be the reserves and have to sit bench. Unconsciously, their wave flow can disrupt the performance of the team on the field. Deep resentments and anger that are not dealt with in a positive way, will lower the powerfulness of the team. It is important that a reserve's thoughts about the team needs to be moulded into the wholeness. Coaches often unconsciously reject or avoid the reserve. The opposite also occurs, with the reserve rejecting the coach. Their waves are clashing even though there is no verbal contact. This may affect the synergy of the team. Take careful note of the body language of the coach and the reserves on the bench, when next watching rugby or soccer on television.

Always being on the bench can erode a player's confidence. A division between team and reserves can occur. Reserves may not feel part of a team, since they have not managed to establish their own position in a team. Since they are not actually playing, they may feel resentful of their fellow team mates. In addition, they do not feel emotionally calm. Some reserves may feel cheated and badly done by, since they may not have been given a chance by the coach.

### Connecting Players — Generating Synergy

There is continual energy interchange between players in a team, and between coach and players. This interchange can be on a verbal or physical level. I always ask members of a team to answer four questions for me (but not to reveal the answers):

1. Which player in the team do they most respect?
2. Which player in the team do they feel most comfortable with?
3. Which player do they most rely on during a match?
4. On a personal level, who do they least know in the team?

It does not matter who each of the individual players have chosen. Let us assume that player X choses players A, B, B, and C in response to questions 1, 2, 3, and 4 respectively. From the perspective of player X, player A is admired. Player A is like a father figure and can provide new learning to player X. I encourage player X to discuss playing issues with player A. In question 2, Player B can provide the necessary emotional support when things get tough. In stressful times, player X is encourged to use this player as a meaningful resource.

Question 3 identifies the vital link that exists between two players on the field during performance. Before a match, it is important that player X and B sit down together and discuss possible concerns regarding performance. In hockey or rugby, for example, it is important for the coach to break up the team into its natural subgroups for in-depth discussion. In hockey, the defenders, the midfield and the forwards offer natural groupings. In rugby, the tight five; the loose forwards; the scrum-half and fly-half; the centres, wings and full-back, are the natural groups. The proper functioning in these subgroups is dependent on each of the individual players understanding who is relying on whom in what situation and what is to be expected from each of the players. This discussion is vital. It strengthens the team connectedness. Each player gains new insight into the links that make up the whole.

Player X and player C are personally least familiar with each other. Under stress, this becomes the weakest link, and will be placed under most strain. In this superficial example, I would encourage player X to spend some time with player C on both a formal and informal level. Just standing next to player C while having a drink will provide player X will more information and understanding of how player C thinks and behaves. While practising, player X should involve himself in activities in which player C is involved. Just hitting balls to each other builds up the relationship and in the process increases the interpersonal strength between the players X and C. This in turn, creates more team synergy. In all of these examples, conscious and unconscious energy exchange is taking place. In the process, a powerful synergy is being woven.

Some healers use touch in order to transfer energy from a higher source to a lower energy level. Psychotherapists are also aware of energy transfer during therapy. Counselling is an exhausting process for the psychologist or helper. At the end of the exchange, the client will feel renewed on some level, if meaningful energy transfer has occurred. During interaction, however, wastage and dissipation of energy can also occur. The experienced counsellor has an intuitive feel of when to say what, during the flow of conversation in order to reduce energy wastage. Too much talking invariably leads to dissipation.

As a coach, it is important to be aware of when to talk, how to talk, and with whom to talk, when interacting with team players. Do not talk and shout for the sake of believing and showing that you are 'coaching'. You may be wasting vital information. Sometimes keeping quiet can be the most powerful message given to the players. Do not be afraid of physical touch. A pat on the back, holding a player on the shoulder, an encouraging hug, are all very important messages. These are powerful relationship builders. Touching, however, needs to be spontaneous and comfortable for both coach and player. What is important to realise, is that energy transfer takes place and relationships strengthened during physical contact. However, it is important to emphasise that this should not be forced.

### Linking Individual, Subgroup and Team

In team sports it is important to link individual, subgroup and team objectives in order to generate synergy. These goals are operating on different levels, and therefore should not in any way clash with each other.

In discussion, players should be given the opportunity to talk about the team. This allows each individual to make comments about his experiences in the team. This process ensures that important concerns about the team may be acknowledged and dealt with.

A healthy functioning team is able to reflect inwards and develop a plan of action to confront any issue or concern that an individual may present. The team must be able to accommodate any individual's concern or perception.

In addition, the team goal should incorporate a strategy for the match, a team tactic. This is the game plan that ties individuals together into a unified whole.

For the 1992 Currie Cup final, the Natal rugby team had to deal with a number of issues. Firstly, they had to remain in the moment and not become past focused regarding the 1990 Currie Cup victory. The team had to understand that the conditions surrounding the 1992 final were totally different from those circumstances operating in the 1990 final. The trap was to believe that these finals were going to be the same.

A team naturally divides into subgroups when it comes to informal groupings. Certain individuals will remain together, and feel comfortable with each other regarding the more private aspects of their lives. This needs to be respected. Ian McIntosh, the Natal coach, allowed the players their own free time and space after supper on the night before the final. This allowed each individual the freedom to be with those people who he felt most comfortable with. This ensured that no negative energy flow occurred between the players in the build-up to the big match.

As part of the intricate web of connections that exist in a team, I broke up the Natal team into natural playing subgroups. Three subgroups emerged; namely the tight forwards, the loose forwards (including scrum-half and fly-half), and the three quarters (back line). As part of the wholeness of a team, the management and coaching subgroup also discussed relevant issues pertaining to their areas of responsibility. Each of these groups had to map out for themselves, relevant objectives for the match. A clear focus of what was to be achieved needed to be discussed. Further, the sub-group had to make positive comments concerning the playing strengths of each of the individuals who were in the subgroup.

On an individual level, each player needs to have a clear focus of his role. I always ask players to focus on a simple goal regarding their performance. Building up to a match, it is important that each individual has a quiet period alone in order to reflect. In particular, this is extremely important when a team is on tour and where players are constantly rubbing shoulders with each other. There may be times when an individual feels as if he is suffocating in the group. Therefore, spending some time alone (creating one's own space), provides an opportunity to get clarity about your own thinking regarding your own performance.

These three levels (individual, subgroup and team), need to be integrated into a unified whole. The integration should not exclude any view or perception that may have been generated on any of the levels.

As an example of this integration, a five-point mental map emerged with the 1992 Natal rugby team:

1. Remain simple in what you do.
2. Use what you have.
3. Focus on an image of commitment and courage, when the going gets tough.
4. This final is a challenge to test the true character of individual and team.
5. This is a special moment.

This created the framework for the generation of synergetic power within the team. Each player becomes linked in a meaningful way. A wholeness emerges that ensures that energy is released in a directed and focus way.

Cricket is an extremely complex game when it comes to looking at the interaction between individual, subgroup and team. For example, while fielding and bowling, the subgroup of bowlers are having to deal with the match demands. Physical effort and a period of sustained mental concentration are required. During this period, other players could help maintain the bowler's focus through emotional support. In this way, the individual fielder can retain the connection between himself and the subgroup of bowlers.

In a discussion with a cricket squad, I made the point that the energy vibes of individuals vary. While some of a bowler's team mates may be able to spark something inside of him while bowling, there may be other players who have the opposite effect. It is important to become sensitive to these feelings. There are some fellow players who naturally make one feel comfortable and motivated. There is just something in their manner that triggers and activates energy flow.

The demands on the different subgroups vary remarkably in cricket. On bowling a side out, the pressure is immediately transferred onto the subgroup of 'upper order batsmen'. Before the final wicket has been taken, it is important that the opening batsmen start mentally preparing. Awareness of pace and bounce of the wicket is vital. Further information about whether the wicket is seaming or the ball swinging can be obtained from one's own bowlers. In addition, the opening batsmen could be going through a visualisation of themselves batting.

During a change of innings, the bowlers will naturally feel relieved and may want to release built-up frustration. This is normal. However, the opening batsmen are emotionally at the opposite end of the scale regarding their focus. It is therefore important that no clash of energy flow occurs. If needs be, the bowlers may need to separate themselves from the opening batsmen and be sensitive to the mental preparation that the opening batsmen may be undertaking.

## *Stamina — Using and Creating Energy*

From the Taoist perspective, Chi (energy) will be flowing within an organism and between people operating in space. Chi transmits patterns. It is not a substance.

> 'The qualitative aspect of Chi lies in its directionality. Quality is the complement to quantity. We are dealing with two aspects of reality: mass, which is static and fixed, which has extension and is accumulated; and movement, which is dynamic and has no extension. Quality, for me, refers to movement, to processes, to functions, or to change.' (Porkert, in discussion with Capra, 1988:172)

Living requires energy. When I think of energy, I think of process and movement. Process and movement incorporate the dimension of time. Human energy is not unlimited and infinite. Energy gets used up in activities.

Here follow some examples of energy use. The human system uses energy internally on digestion. Worries, conflicts and problems use up mental energy as a person tries to resolve the issues. This mental strain may result in a feeling of lethargy in the body. Symptoms of depression, for example, include disinterest in sex, always wanting to sleep, the loss of appetite. Even eating seems to take up too much energy. The completion of a work project that requires intensive work at the computer will in time result in tiredness.

Playing a five-set international squash match will require intensive explosive physical energy release in a short time period; while a cricket test match requires a slower release of energy, depending on whether you are a batsman or bowler.

In the July 1991 edition of *Red* magazine, I stated that the most important impetus for endurance is if you value something or if you have found meaning in a situation that you are involved in. If the mind creates meaning in a situation and there is a high level of interest in the activity, then energy flow can be maintained for longer periods.

However, doing the same activity over and over again uses up the same type of energy. Sameness depletes energy quickly. Energy is generated by situations that provide varied stimulation.

In other words, regeneration of energy requires a variety of activities that complement each other. Difference in types of activity, ensure longer periods of directed energy flow. While studying, for example, it is important to break the activity. Mixing physical activity with study periods creates the balance to allow for longer utilisation of the energy in concentration.

> 'One cannot enjoy doing the same thing at the same level for long. We grow either bored or frustrated; and then the desire to enjoy ourselves again pushes us to stretch our skills, or to discover new opportunities for using them.' (Csikszentmihalyi, 1991, quoted in *The Star*)

With regard to stress and burnout, things start going wrong when too much emphasis and focus is being placed in one area, with too much intensity. For example, if you push too hard for too long in business, you will start slowing down. If you do not pick up the cues (in both mind and body), and just keep on pushing, you may suffer burnout. It is like driving a car with your foot flat on the accelerator without changing gear or considering the terrain in which you are driving. There are two possible consequences in such a situation; either you crash or the car engine seizes and has a blow-out.

One should never separate mind and body. The biggest cause of burnout in sport is when athletes have the will to keep on pushing and seem to have more stamina for a while. Yet in time, they drop off substantially in performance. Marathon running is an obvious example where a lot of physical damage can result from a person's ability to cut off the mind from the body. In building up to running marathons coaches often warn novice runners about doing too much, too quickly, in too short a time.

The natural replenishers of energy are rest, relaxation and sleep. A further dimension on the generation and utilisation of energy is the principle of balance and understanding the nature of flow.

> 'There seem to be two kinds of activity — activity in harmony with nature and activity against the natural flow of things.' (Capra, 1982:20)

Taoism offers the concept of non-action. This should not be interpreted as a passive acceptance of a problem. Instead, non-action refers to abstaining from activities that go against the grain of things. Sometimes one wastes energy by pushing against the wall, despite intuitively feeling that the action is not resulting in the desired outcome. Non-action is the opposite to forced-action. Non-action understands that timing is a very important factor in unleashing creative energy. Non-action considers the type of conditions that prevail in a situation; and responds according to those factors that are operating at that moment.

## QUANTUM LEAPS — PERFECT TIMING TO PEAK

The ideas presented in the previous sections, and in the chapters on Mind in Action and The Psychology of Winning, need to be kept in mind while covering this section. An integration of concepts is necessary. It is in the integration of these ideas that the phenomenon of quantum leaps or peak performance exists.

Bruce Fordyce has been a master in being able to peak at the right time for a race (in this case, the Comrades). 'If I have got a big race coming up, I plan for it. The thing with ultra-marathons is that you don't race every week-end, maybe two or three in a year. The way you do it is that you will train hard for a specific period. As the race gets nearer you cut back on the training. You become lighter, and stronger, and rested, and keen to race,' said Bruce.

'So you would have to hold yourself back, in order to feel strong to go forward?' I asked. 'Yes, physically hold myself back. And then mentally...I don't race too often so I feel like racing when I go and race. I know from past experience that if I race a lot, I get tired of it. In the race itself, I hold back. If you are going to run 90km to go screaming off in the front right in the beginning must be the most stupid thing you could do,' comments Bruce.

Boxing and ultra-marathon running are very much alike, in that one should only compete two or three times a year. Both sports are physically and mentally draining. The build-up to the event takes careful planning and monitoring with regards to training. Brian

Mitchell's training peaked ten days before the actual fight. He then organised a 12 four-minute round gym fight with three sparring partners. After this, he cut back on his physical training, yet still carefully monitored his weight. Brian could obtain valuable inner messages about both his physical and mental condition for the upcoming fight, from the way he responded in the gym fight. This gave him confidence. He also knew that his body needed ten days to recover, in order for him to be at his energetic best for the title fight.

In discussion with Bruce and Brian, it was apparent that they were highly tuned into their own energy flow. By consciously holding himself back in a race, Bruce gives himself the best opportunity to move forward with directed purpose. Brian peaked his training ten days before the fight in order to be in peak condition for the fight. Both these sportsmen had worked out unique programmes for themselves. They knew what it took in training to be able to peak at the exact time. They also knew when to stop training. This is the most important information that an athlete needs to know about himself: when to push forward and when to hold back; how much to extend during practice and when to accept the limitations of self.

The power in performance comes when action fits the conditions that prevail. The timing is of great importance. It is like knowing when to catch the right wave. It may be necessary to let waves go by, in order to be ready for the one that you want. This takes patience. A bigger picture is perceived. Waves are not viewed as being single entities; instead, a wholeness emerges. Purposeful action that fits in the moment, results in a spontaneous release of energy. No force is evident.

### Synchronisation in Rowing

The process of getting a team to become a team, can be taxing and at times emotional. It takes time to mould a powerful whole. In order to attain a holistic harmony, each individual has to confront his own individual beliefs and prejudices regarding the group.

In my consulting with the South African lightweight rowing crew, I knew that it was vital that the rowers achieve a oneness in the boat if they were to achieve the success they were capable of. In the initial stages of the mental preparation, the crew felt that there was no group harmony and togetherness. This was natural and to be expected with a new crew. The difficulty in achieving this harmony in the boat was largely due to oarsmen from different clubs being selected to represent South Africa in one boat. Eight individual differences needed to be integrated into a harmonious whole. The power of the crew depended on the commitment that each oarsman made to the harmonious working of the group. The more that one individual unconsciously went against the group flow, the more disruption and the less the harmony in the whole. The nature or personality of the group, is always determined by the attitudes of the individuals to each other.

The process of achieving this wholeness or oneness takes time. Relationships develop over time. Being in one boat, part of one crew, is a fundamental concept that all rowers understand. A unifying theme of 'we are all in the same boat' is a clear statement that reflects the core value of interdependence and togetherness of rowing.

Rowing is a sport that requires perfect synchronisation of energy flow. One South African rower spoke about the 'hum' of the boat when the crew's synergy had reached a new level. The boat is propelled with effortless effort. Unlike other sports, rowing cannot afford any individual to be out of line with the rhythm of the whole. Yet, the rhythm of the whole is determined by the activity of flow of each individual. Individual and whole are cybernetically linked. The individual and crew are constantly feeding into each other, and in the process affecting or influencing one another. Individual is picking up the movement of the boat, yet is also contributing to this rhythm.

Oneness occurs when perfect harmony is achieved by all the crew members. A rower stated that one can just feel it in the boat if the whole has not merged as one. Although each individual mind operates and responds differently, the rower must be able to mould this difference (in his unique way) into directed crew sameness. Like a laser beam, the power of the beam is the result of concentrated sameness of light wave energy.

A crew of eight can be thought of as a series of chain links, with each crew member having someone in front and behind him. These make up the front, middle and behind, series of links. There is overlap across the links. A crew member who is in front for one link, is in the middle of another link, and behind for yet another link. Each rower picks up the activity flow of the crew members immediately in front and behind him. If there is disrupted activity flow (consciously or unconsciously, mentally or physically) in any link, this will get transferred throughout the crew in a matter of five strokes.

The cox is part of the crew interaction by virtue of his verbal connection with them. He is the observer, yet is not separate from that what is being observed (he is on the boat, and is part of the crew momentum). He gives information about the nature of the rhythm of activity of the crew. He comments on whether rushing is occurring (trying to row too quickly in the hope of going faster). The cox is like a coach. He must therefore become aware of whether he may be inadvertently increasing the disruption of the crew. He must articulate critical moments during the race in the form of messages or comments given at the appropriate time.

### Northern Transvaal Dominance — A New Rule?

Over time a pattern of interaction also emerges between two opposing teams. As an example, I will highlight the relationship between the Northern Transvaal and Natal rugby teams. Before the 6th October 1990, the pattern of expectation of the end result was predictable. Northern Transvaal were extremely dominant with Natal willing to be submissive. This type of relationship gets shaped over time, and is initially due to real playing strengths and weaknesses of the players from the provinces.

Over time, the historical nature of this relationship shapes matches that occur in the present. A predictable pattern starts emerging. In the two league matches leading up to the 1990 Currie Cup final, this pattern continued with Northern Transvaal convincing winners 24–9 (played at Kings Park) and 28–6 (played at Loftus Versfeld). The status quo was being maintained. The only way to break the pattern, is to generate a quantum leap to a new level.

One of the many complex ingredients for a peak performance is the balance between relaxation and arousal. When I first made contact with the Natal rugby team three days before the 1990 Currie Cup final, it was important that unnecessary concern and worry (energy) should not be wasted in the days leading up to the final. If the players got aroused too soon, valuable energy would dissipate. The power of the team will then be reduced. It was therefore necessary to incorporate periods of quiet reflection and relaxation in the mental preparation of the team to the final.

In the Currie Cup final, Natal were able to unleash and utilise their directed energy against Northern Transvaal. There was a quantum leap in performance that shocked and amazed rugby enthusiasts. The 'impossible' was achieved.

After this event, a new pattern of interaction on the rugby field has emerged between these two provinces. In the 1991 rugby season, Natal outplayed Northern Transvaal to win both Currie Cup league matches, 54–15 (at Kings Park) and 22–12 (at Loftus Versfeld). To date (Oct 1992), the teams have clashed again at Loftus Versfeld on 17 May 1992, with Northern Transvaal running out as winners 27–24. All the points came from the boot of fly-half, Naas Botha. On the 27 June 1992, Natal again beat Northerns 17–12 at Kings Park. In the matches to come, I expect that these two teams will continue to excite supporters and the media, as they grapple with their new rugby relationship.

### The Final Hurdle

A pattern also exists between a team and the ground at which they play. Certain stadiums make players feel uncomfortable, while other grounds seem to pull out the best in the players. Over time, a particular ground may take on a 'hoodoo' meaning for a team. Over time the side may always under-perform in that context. Breaking that pattern may not be achieved through verbal self-assurance; a quantum leap in thinking is needed, in order to 'free' the team from being kept hostage by the ground.

A sporting season usually culminates in teams having to play in a final. There are teams that are able to reach the final fairly consistently over time, but seem to choke in the situation. A self-fulfilling pattern emerges. Unconsciously, the players that have to confront the moment (playing in the final), also have to deal with the historical pattern of always having failed at the final hurdle. This does not allow for the players to operate freely in the moment, with 'no mind', and with creative energy flow. Unconsciously, the players may just 'know' that this final may not be any different. In other words, the players may verbally state that they are confident of winning the final, yet unconsciously have to deal with the pressures of the past historical pattern. This is a theme that needs to be dealt with if the team is to make a quantum leap to a new level.

Before the 1992 Barcelona Olympics, the Australian hockey men's team had never won an Olympic medal. It was a known fact that the team always 'choked' in the final matches, after the round robin pool series of matches. They always tended to play below their potential in those important matches. According to hockey critics, the players tended to be over-anxious, which caused them to freeze in those matches.

After the pool matches in the 1992 Olympics, Australia had ended first in their section with Germany second. The pool match between these two teams resulted in an evenly contested 1–1 draw. In the other section, Pakistan finished first, with Holland in second place. The two semi-finals were Australia versus Holland and Pakistan versus Germany.

In the match against Holland the Australian team played their usual pattern of high energy hockey that put a great deal of pressure on the Dutch. The Australians closed down space quickly, high into the opposition's half. The match ended in a 3–2 win for the Australians. This put the Australians through to the finals, and assured them of a silver medal at worst. In the other semi-final, the Germans beat Pakistan 1–0.

Before the final, the Australian team came out onto the field 45 minutes before the start. The players looked relaxed, yet seemed to be somewhat casual and care-free in the manner in which they warmed up. I remarked to Dr Ken West (vision consultant for the South African men's hockey team) that I thought that the players were 'acting' relaxed. For example, for both the semi-final and this match, the whole team did a loosening activity ('breaking the ice' type of activity), in which the players stand in a circle and throw a soft ball around. Catching and throwing the ball, with verbal chatter in between, provided the opportunity for the players to unwind. The only significant difference in the execution of this simple game for the semi-final and now for the final, was that the ball was dropped by one or other player after about two to three throws. The players ambled off casually, while retrieving the dropped ball. The game just did not get off the ground. It seemed that their minds were everywhere, but on this activity. Maybe the players were preoccupied with what was to come. The activity just did not seem to fit.

Even while warming up their basics, Ken West felt that the players were not grooving their biomechanics in a focused way. Hitting and stopping skills were being performed without the necessary concentration and commitment. Observing from the outside, it just seemed that the players had the wrong impression of what the feeling of relaxed focusedness actually feels like. This may have been due to their never having experienced the correct balance between arousal and relaxation.

Surprising to many spectators, the Australians also changed their familiar playing style and instead tried to play a waiting game against the Germans. Maybe the management and players had wanted to prove to themselves that they could be relaxed in an important match. Being relaxed may have become an issue (it certainly seemed that way during the activity that I have outlined). Within the first minute of the match, the Germans had scored. At half-time (1–0 to Germany), the Australian players seemed despondent and frustrated. There was very little communication between the players. It was as if the players had felt that they had failed. It was common knowlegde from the press reports that the Australians were determined to break the 'hoodoo' of never having achieved an Olympic medal. However, it had seemed that the team had wanted more. It was going to be gold or nothing.

In watching the body language of the Australian players, I thought to myself what I would have said to the players at that stage. I felt it would be necessary to free the thinking of the players. I would have made two comments. Firstly, I would have asked the players if they were enjoying themselves. If they answered negatively, I would have ascertained what factors were blocking or stopping them from enjoying the moment. Acknowledging and making these factors overt, often results in a feeling of relief. Secondly, I would have stated that the worst that could possibly happen would be to win the silver medal, and at this moment they had achieved what no other Australian team were able to do. They had made history and I was proud of them. These comments would have been aimed at trying to release the trapped energy.

Five minutes into the second half the Germans scored again. Immediately after this goal, there was a 15-minute period where Australia dominated. Unfortunately, they were not able to convert this pressure into scoring a goal. The final score was 2–1 to Germany, with the Australians having scored in the last five minutes of the match.

I know that coming second hurts the inner pride. But even when receiving their silver medals, the Australian players seemed so unhappy. In their minds they had defined themselves as failures. In their minds they may have felt that they had again choked in an important match. This is an issue that will need careful thought in the Australian camp. History can build up internal pressure which then interferes with the energy flow in the present; past encroaches on the present.

### Peak Synergy in Ice Hockey

In March 1992, I was involved in the mental preparation of the South African Ice Hockey team for the World Cup, group C, competition. I moved with the energy flow of the team in its build-up to the competition, as well as between the five test matches during the tournament. Besides covering the usual aspects of mental preparation through visualisation, relaxation, dealing with stress, and focusing on the game plan, I was acutely aware that the team was a living organism in flow over time. Energy was the fuel for expectations in mind and activity on the ice. It became vital that energy on all levels needed to be utilised and directed both on a conscious and unconscious level.

The side made a remarkable start to the competition, with a convincing victory against Luxembourg (23–0). The match produced a connected directionality of qualitative flow. After the match, players expressed comments that reflected a quantum leap experience. In such experiences, integration of mind and body energy occurs without force or effort. In matches such as these, all the individual energies jell together. A feeling of oneness emerges — everything fits together as time unfolds — nothing goes wrong.

This test match reminded me of the wonderful World Cup cricket debut of the South African side against Australia in February 1992. Maybe these peak performances were due to the long awaited re-entry into international sport. We were hungry. We wanted to do well. There was an inner urgency to show the world. This provides a great deal of physical and mental energy in a team that is just waiting to be unleashed.

## The After Effects

It is always difficult for a coach to know how to deal with the after-effects of such a high. The next match always tests the physical and mental resilience of the team. In the preparation for the next match, players are still unconsciously connected to the past match, despite being verbally told by the coach to prepare fully in mind and body for the match to come.

Unconsciously, the players and coach hanker for a re-experience. Those feelings of exhilaration that were experienced become the very obstacle in obtaining a clear focus for the next match to come. Unfortunately, the players become past-orientated in order to recapture the ease of flow during that remarkable match. They no longer operate in nowness.

It takes time for an individual to recover from the release of intense energy. Regeneration of mental and physical energy cannot be switched on, as one does when switching on a light. There are natural time periods and processes that operate. In international competitions that cover a limited time period (say three weeks in which eight matches are played), the athlete is continually being expected to regenerate quicker than the natural process may allow.

Paradoxically, in sport, nature's way to trigger the quickest regeneration of creative energy is through poor performance and set-back. In the World Cup cricket tournament, the outstanding win against Australia was followed by losses against New Zealand and then Sri Lanka. At that point, the players must have been faced with the harsh reality that their hopes of reaching the semi-final were dwindling. This seemed to generate revival. The team then showed remarkable character in beating the West Indies and the eventual winners, Pakistan.

### Linking High and Low

The next ice hockey test was against Turkey, and despite winning 18–1 the players did not feel the ease of flow as experienced in the previous match (past orientated focus that is unavoidable). 'Frustration', 'disruption' and 'no rhythm' were used to describe their experiences of the match. 'The feel in the change-room was different' was a comment from a senior player. At this stage, it was important to become re-connected in the present, and deal with the energy flow that was available. Three questions were posed to the players:

1. What is your thinking at the moment? (nowness)
2. Comments on what you have learnt during the past two tests? (how the past shapes the present)
3. Individual and team objectives still to achieve? (from nowness to shaping the future)

In the team's discussion of these questions, it was evident that the players were struggling to make sense of the contrasting feelings that they had experienced in the two test matches (despite the convincing wins). It was important for me to outline to the team, that energy flow over time moves in upward and downward cycles. The tremendous energy release after the Luxembourg test resulted in a feeling of flatness in the Turkey match. This is normal. This is how nature operates. This awareness seemed to result in an acceptance and relaxedness in the team. The belief that the team was complacent and not motivated for the Turkey match was given new meaning. At this point, expectations for future action could now be discussed. A new focus for the next test match was outlined. Unconscious and conscious energy was free to flow.

The next two tests were challenges in their own right, presenting the team with other issues to deal with. In the process new insights and learning took place. The test match against Greece highlighted the phenomenon of energy flow in more complexity. The ice rink was jam-packed with supporters. The Greek support comprised about 25% of the crowd, yet was able to generate 75% of the noise and activity. The Greek supporters were unified in motion and directed in action (vocal support). An electrifying atmosphere was being created for the start of the match. The South African supporters were unable to generate any motion. They were frozen. The Greek players unconsciously sensed this and came out highly charged. Within 90 seconds the South African team were two goals down. Our team had also become frozen. The ability to yield in the face of directed force is necessary in a situation such as this. In time, the team had the ability to re-direct the force in order to achieve the objective that they had focused on. The result, a 9–4 victory.

## The Unconscious Connection

At this stage, the South African team had played four tests and were unbeaten. Spain was in the same position. A top of the table clash was now a reality. In line with our programme, a mental training workshop was arranged for the day before the test against Spain.

It is not always practical for me to attend all the matches that are played by teams with whom I have consulted. When I do attend matches, I prefer to keep some physical distance from the activity of the team, in the build-up at the start of a match. While sitting in the crowd, I can observe play from my perspective. I remain consciously connected to the team and each of the individual players during the process of play. I take note of how the discussion in the mental training session (which was conducted before the match), links with the activity on the field, in other words, how ideas and action connect.

I had missed only one test match in the series (played against Israel, which we had won). I had moved with the team over time, and had become aware of the issues and concerns of the team. I was connected to the team and had enjoyed watching the action-packed excitement of ice hockey. For the Spanish test, however, I had a pre-arranged management seminar that had been organised for the same day. I would not be able to watch the test match. I was not happy about this, but unfortunately, could not change pre-arranged commitments.

In our mental preparation workshop, I did not feel it necessary to tell the players that I would not be watching the match, especially since I believe that a team has its own healthy drive to succeed. Their success is not dependent on my attending the match. As we consciously prepared for the match ahead, I did not feel inwardly comfortable. It was as if something was missing. What would the effects be of my not being at the match, I started to wonder? This was an extremely unusual thought. Would this disconnection affect the connectedness in the team? I started to think about the unconscious connections and their influence on the team synergy. These were some of my inner doubts during the mental preparation. I am sure that some of these 'vibes' were being transmitted (how and in what form is never known) to the team.

I believe that the power of a team's directed energy is determined by the nature of the interpersonal connectedness in the team and between my own connectedness with the team and the specific individuals. Team and individual operate on different levels. The directed energy release in mind and body of each individual determines the quality of the team. If there are any unconscious blockages in the minds of the individuals, the quality of the directed energy would be reduced. Unconscious conflicts or interpersonal issues consume energy in the individual and team's quest to seek balance and harmony. Being part of the team, I was aware that this also applied to me. A coach or a sports psychologist cannot separate their own inner worries from that of the team.

In presenting the management seminar, I felt totally disconnected. There was no flow. I consciously attempted to concentrate, yet unconsciously I must still have being connected to the team in the test match being played. Unconsciously, I was not prepared for this management context. I was not totally in the moment. It seemed as if I was being torn apart. My own energy flow was being fragmented. I stumbled over words, and felt that I was not making sense in the discussion. It was a strange sensation.

Relationships are sensitive to unconscious energy flow. I had experienced a split or fragmentation within myself. I therefore wondered if my own feelings at the management seminar, had in some way affected the team (despite the separation in distance). I will never know what effect (if any) my absence had on the team's performance. In discussion with the coach, he felt that the team was too tight during the match. This resulted in too many unforced errors. Further, he did feel that we had been beaten by a more professional and competent Spanish team.

It is important to understand that a context of interpersonal relationships exist between individuals that make up the team (including coach and sports psychologist) that transcend space and time. To add further complexity, I would like to make some comments regarding my involvement with the 1990 and 1992 Natal Currie Cup champions, and my physical attendance at matches.

While I attended the match in person at Loftus Versfeld (and thoroughly enjoyed the tremendous atmosphere), I experienced a inner need to remain alone and quiet for the 1992 final (this surfaced on the day of the final while I was actually getting dressed to go to Ellis Park). Although I had tickets to the match, I decided that I would rather remain at home and watch the match on television. In making this decision, I did not feel any inner turmoil or disconnection. In fact, I felt the exact opposite. It seemed to fit for me.

The unconscious connections that exist in a team are made up of all the feelings, thoughts, attitudes of the individuals that make up the whole. Each person (including coach and sports psychologist) needs to be at peace with himself in the way that he connects to the group, and then to understand that these feelings or thoughts may be moving with or against the team flow. Destructive individual thoughts concerning other team members, will reduce the synergy in a team.

I have used myself as an example to convey the true essence of relationship connection. I contend that one's own inner feelings can influence the flow and performance of the whole. Relationship connections transcend space. Minds are linked despite distance.

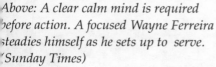

*Above: A clear calm mind is required before action. A focused Wayne Ferreira steadies himself as he sets up to serve. (Sunday Times)*

*Above right: In perfect balance, the performance of Heidi Marie Oosthuizen reflects a well-'grooved' body in interaction with a relaxed and calm mind. (Oosthuizen)*

*Right: Jimmy Cook remains simple in action in the initial stage of his innings in order to build a platform for ease of flow in scoring later on. (Beeld)*

*Left: Striving for quality in action during practice — in perfect balance, an airborne Jonty Rhodes unleashes a throw while working on his fielding. (Sunday Times)*

*Opposite page, top: Ray Jennings, a fitness fanatic who strives for a culture of excellence through dedicated effort in training. He holds the South African wicketkeeping record for most first-class dismissals. (Author)*

*Below: Lift-off! A feeling of lightness in body can be attained through visualisation. Charmaine Weavers, the South African record-holder in the women's high jump, seems suspended in mid-air at the zenith of her jump. (Beeld)*

*Left: Peaking for world title fights requires hours and hours of carefully planned training. Brian Mitchell developed a unique training pro-gramme to get mind and body into top shape for his fights. (Beeld)*

*Above: A body in motion with no time to think. James Small, the South African wing, flies past a diving opponent. (Sunday Times)*

*Left: Directing energy into explosive action — a focused Allan Donald in full flight. (Beeld)*

*Above: The short corner setpiece demands intense concentration from players. Rob Pullen is about to explode out of the goals, while Gregor Maier (goalkeeper), Warren Bond and Wayne Graham gear themselves for action. (Author)*

*Below: A balance between attack and defence is vital in boxing. Brian Mitchell, the undefeated World Junior Lightweight champion, finds a critical opening in the defence of his opponent. (Beeld)*

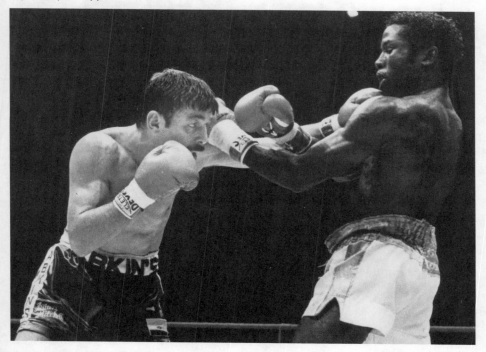

Top: Half-time is a period to refocus on the team's objectives. An intense Jannie Breedt, the Transvaal captain, outlines a definite plan of action to his players in the 1992 Currie Cup final against Natal. (Sunday Times)

Bottom: A critical moment at half-time in the rugby test against the All Blacks, as captain Naas Botha leaves the group. (Sunday Times)

*A dynamic balance between relaxation and focused concentration is necessary. Taking time out from the intensity of competition, Lee Trevino and Severiano Ballesteros share a humorous moment. (Beeld)*

*In highly interactive team sports such as rugby and soccer, individual stress is heightened when there is no support in the space around the ball.*

*Top: Tony Watson, Dick Muir and Andrew Blakeway of Natal create a 3-on-1 situation during the 1992 Currie Cup final against Transvaal.*
*(Sunday Times)*

*Bottom : Isolated from his team, 'Chippa' Masinga has to cope with three Zambians during the African Cup soccer qualifier. South Africa lost 0–1.*
*(Sunday Times)*

*Above: A partnership of shared responsibility. A determined Brian Mitchell, in training with coach Harold Volbrectht.*
*(Sunday Times)*

*Left: Coaches are under stress to get players to perform according to a tactical game plan. Stanley 'Screamer' Tshabalala, the ex-South African soccer coach, vents his frustration.*
*(Sunday Times)*

*Below: The Comrades Marathon, the ultimate test of physical endurance and mental toughness. A determined Bruce Fordyce, followed by Mark Page, on the way to setting an up-run record of 5 hr 27 min 42 sec in the 1988 Comrades Marathon. (Beeld)*

*Left: The end of a tough journey — a triumphant Willie Engelbrecht, winner of the 1990 Rapport and 1992 Argus cycling tours, gives the 'thumbs up'. (Beeld)*

*Below: Team synergy creates a feeling of wellbeing for players, especially after a demanding contest that has ended in victory. The 1992 Currie Cup champions, Natal. (Sunday Times)*

*Above, top: An embrace that reflects the true camaraderie of sport. Ian McIntosh, the Natal rugby coach, and Jannie Breedt, Transvaal captain, share an emotional moment after an exhausting contest in the 1992 Currie Cup final. Natal won 14–13. (Sunday Times)*

*Above, bottom: The sweet taste of a historic victory — Craig Jamieson, captain of the 1990 Natal rugby team, drinks from the Currie Cup after defeating Northern Transvaal 18–12 at Loftus Versfeld. (Beeld)*

## CHAPTER 4

# The ecology and psychology of coaching

Coaching is a complex human endeavour that is embedded in relationships. To coach means to impart knowledge to an athlete in such a way as to ensure that the athlete develops his skills. Coaching implies helping and guiding.

If the athlete is to benefit from the coaching process, the coach must be able to create the sort of learning context that allows for open discussion and problem solving.

Gaining respect as a coach, depends on how the athlete perceives the relationship that exists. Respect is linked to honesty, support, communication and trust. This chapter provides a framework to examine your own beliefs and attitudes regarding the coaching process. The ideas that I will be sharing challenge the traditional view that 'coaches know best'.

In particular, I believe that it is important to reflect upon the assumptions that one makes in the process of thinking, while operating in a coaching context.

Besides dealing with technical and tactical information, the focus of a coach should always be on the coaching relationship. The coach provides one side to that relationship. Therefore, the coach needs to become aware of himself while trying to impart knowledge to the athlete. The coach becomes part of the coaching and learning process. He is not separate from this process. He does not stand apart from any difficulties that emerge. Instead, the coach becomes part of the problem. There is no reason to blame the athlete for not listening and learning. Rather, the coach should try and understand what he has done to impede learning. The coaching and learning processes are one. The inability to learn is linked to the inability to coach.

### Think about your Thinking

Thinking determines behaviour. Thinking directs energy flow. Thinking allows for certain action, while excluding other considerations.

There has been a shift in the type of thinking in the scientific world, as new complex global difficulties emerge. Our old ways of problem-solving are proving to be useless, as we enter into the 21st century. In order to respond to these problems, a new vision of reality, with fundamental changes in thought, perception, expectation, and values is necessary (Capra, 1982). A new paradigm (way of thinking) needs to emerge. This will require us to give up our simplistic, quantitative science, and learn to think as nature thinks (Bateson, 1979).

Systemic ecological thinking has emerged to deal with the global issues of AIDS, pollution, population explosion, exploitation of natural resources and urbanisation. These problems confront the mechanistic world view of problem resolution. In fact, it has been man's arrogance in believing that he is able to dictate and control his environment for his own selfish needs that has resulted in these problems and in his own isolation. His old thinking patterns no longer offer resolution of the emerging global difficulties.

Systemic thinking emerges when a person focuses on the abused world that now exists, and understands that complex, interdependent relationships in the fabric of life are being threatened (Beck and Linscott, 1991). The systemic thinker knows that he is connected to this unfolding process and has a need to make sense of this process.

In order to create a framework to examine this more closely, it is necessary to compare two major types of thinking, as was outlined by Auwerswald at a workshop in 1990. The table below compares the old traditional Newtonian thinking (Rules of Mechologic), with the new systemic thinking of connectedness and interdependence (Principles of Ecologic).

| Rules of Mechologic | Principles of Ecologic |
|---|---|
| Single fixed reality | Multiple evolving realities |
| Objectivity | No objective experience |
| Linear time | Space-time |
| Hierarchy | Human participation |
| Mechanical form | Pattern emergence, connection |
| Understanding by analysis | Understanding by context |
| Linear causal process | Circularity |
| Rule of certainty | Paradox |
| Dualism (either/or) | Conversation of ideas (both/and) |
| Name as thing | Map is not the territory |

## Formal Education – The Source of Linear Thinking

Schools and academic institutions teach mechologic where linear cause and effect, quantitative analysis, the seeking of objective truth, and dualist thought processes are emphasised. The rules of mechologic reflect certainty of thinking. Linear analytical thinking processes are at the core of problem solving. There is also the belief that an objective reality exists where everyone sees and feels the same thing at the same time. Further, there is an assumption of hierarchy regarding information flow. For example, the coach is regarded as having more power, because of higher status.

The thorough exploration of this paradigm is beyond the scope of this book. While this paradigm has a place in coaching, and should not be excluded (otherwise this will result in dualist thinking), the main thrust of this chapter is to focus on the principles of ecologic as they apply to coaching in a sports context. In particular, the objective of this chapter is to challenge the assumptions of your thinking.

Whereas Chapter 1 looked at the mind of the athlete before and during performance, this chapter is directed mostly at the coach and his own thinking in interaction with players. In a sense, this chapter provides the foundation for 'The Psychology of Coaching'. I believe that the principles of ecologic are at the core of creative and successful coaching of elite sportsmen. A quantum leap in thinking is needed in order to provide a quantum leap in performance or action.

Systemic thinking will require you to make an intellectual leap. You will have to unlearn the traditional ways of thinking that formal school and university have imposed. You may also have to unlearn some of the traditions that your family or culture imposed on you. This is the challenge that faces all of us, as we develop more complexity in thinking. One needs to constantly question one's assumptions in the process of thinking. Ecologic is a philosophy of how life operates. It presents a pattern of thinking that is in line with how nature functions. Coaching from this perspective is exciting.

## THE ECOLOGY OF COACHING

I now wish to explore in more depth the key ideas, that make up the ecology of coaching. You may notice as you read further that I attempt to challenge your fundamental ideas concerning coaching. I believe that the coach should always examine his own beliefs, ideas, values about sporting situations that he finds himself in. If things go wrong, a coach needs to look inward before blaming players.

### Multiple Views

It is always interesting to gather the opinions of the players in a team after a match. Although one match may have been played, a variety of experiences has resulted. Each player experienced a unique reality during the match and each has created a unique explanation of this reality.

There is no single, fixed objective reality. Instead, there are multiple evolving realities. We are sculptors. We are all constructing and creating our own reality. How these realities connect together is determined by the differences and similarities between the opinions of the individuals. Some opinions clash due to the extreme differences that may emerge. Alternatively, interpersonal comfort occurs when common ground exists between views.

The introduction of the coach's perceptions adds a further reality. In other words, each player, as well as the coach, will be focusing on different issues and/or concerns regarding the match that has unfolded. So which experience is the 'real' truthful one? Which events or explanations should be ignored? I believe that all realities need to be understood and all experiences need to be acknowledged.

The main responsibility of a coach is to integrate and connect the differences that may exist. In the process, a directed group will develop. Respect and tolerance for individual differences is necessary. Despite these differences, the sole objective of each individual in a group should be to focus on his individual task that will ensure group synergy. This will only occur if each individual feels part of the group. The process in getting individuals committed to a group, is to accept and acknowledge each specific perception of the situation that has been experienced.

In describing any event, one always draws distinctions. There is an internal dividing line in mind. A demarcation is drawn. This line of demarcation is unconsciously 'fixed' in the mind. In order to expand one's thinking to new insights, it is necessary to be able to shift this line of demarcation. As this occurs, new distinctions are established and new complexity is introduced.

A comment of: 'You played well' has been arrived at by applying a set of internal criteria in a given situation. 'You played well' also implies that on the other side of the established internal criteria, the mind has decided where 'You did not play well' should be placed. In other words, each person has an internal measuring stick that decides what actions represent 'played well', as opposed to 'not played well'.

A further complication may exist when a coach communicates 'You played well' to an athlete. The lines of demarcation for coach and athlete may be different. Therefore, the internal criteria that judges performance is different. In the athlete's mind he may feel that he did not play well. His standards of performance may be different from those of the coach. The areas of focus vary. The athlete may therefore disagree with the coach's message, or may feel that the coach is not honest.

It is important to discuss the line of demarcation with the athlete. The coach and athlete need to talk about the criteria that they

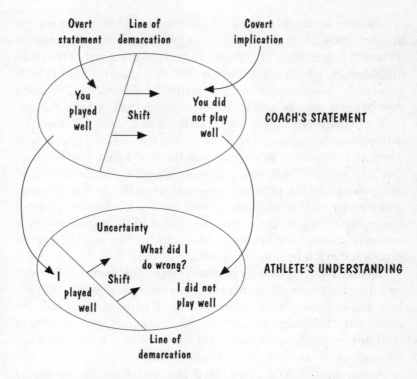

*Figure 15: The lines of demarcation vary from person to person*
          *'You played well' will be defined and interpreted differently*

are using when evaluating performance. I personally prefer using the athlete's line of demarcation and then to redirect or shift his focus. In this way, one uses the familiar criteria or standards of the athlete to get him to learn more about his own performance (as opposed to imposing a view that may be resented or rejected).

In discussion, a provincial hockey player asked me what one should do about a bad umpiring decision during a match, since this caused internal disruption and frustration. There were two aspects to this question. Firstly it depends on which side you are whether a decision is 'good' or 'bad'. If you interpret a decision as being bad, you can rest assured that your opponent perceived that same decision as being right or good.

The second part to the issue under discussion, was the individual response to the player's subjective judgement that the decision was 'bad'. This resulted in his losing his focus on the task that he had set out for himself. The impact of the 'bad' decision should be considered on two levels. Firstly, the opposition tend to become energised and motivated if a decision is perceived to be in their favour. Their performance picks up. Coupled with this, is the downward trend that the player experiences in his own game.

### Be Careful – Do Not Trap Yourself

Natural difficulties or troughs in sporting performance are often misinterpreted and mismanaged by both the coach and athlete. This then leads to an escalation of the problem. Magnification and rigidity of the problem occurs. As a coach, be aware of how you are perceiving and thinking of your players' performance. What do you wish to focus on? How will this affect your problem attack? In what way would you like to intervene? When would the intervention be most suitable? Remember that problem and solution are connected in a circular way. The way you define the problem only allows for a certain possible solution (which may not be the solution!).

Let me expand: I was approached by a hockey coach to help the forwards become 'more aggressive' in order to score goals. In discussion with the coach, it became apparent that she perceived the forwards were not showing enough aggression in shooting at goals. When I enquired as to how she tried to solve the problem, she outlined a whole series of sophisticated exercises in which she tried to generate more aggression in the forwards. Unfortunately, the solution had the opposite effect.

Where previously, the side was still managing to score one or two goals in a match, they now found themselves being unable to convert any opportunities into goals. They were stuck. In the process, the problem was being escalated by the attempted solution. Being disciplined and dedicated, both coach and players continued with 'more of the same' in practice. Unfortunately, performance declined.

In talking to the team, I became aware that the players had become desperate about trying to score goals. As they approached the opposition's goal, they tightened and became too direct in the quest to score. If this team was to overcome their psychological difficulty of not being able to score, they had to 'stop' being so desperate and aggressive about it. They had to relax more while on attack.

During a relaxation, I asked the players to obtain images of aggression. They were asked to draw these images. These were put on the wall, and the players were told to walk around and look at the different images of aggression that exist in the team. In the process, there was a lot of laughter and release of built-up tension, as the players intermingled informally.

To create further understanding of their problem, and to introduce new possible solutions, I asked the players to now create images of situations that represent calmness. As the players were drawing these images, a sense of internal relief was emerging in the team. In further discussions, the team started to generate new solutions to the difficulty of not scoring. The defenders commented that they intended to verbally encourage the forwards. Being supportive, instead of increasing the panic was the underlying message. The forwards developed the phrases 'relaxed composure is the essence of attack' and 'in order to go forward, take a step back'.

In order for the team to break the rigid mind-set of the problem of not scoring goals, it was important for all the players (defenders and forwards) as well as the coach to relax and stop feeding into the attempted solution of trying to become more aggressive. A dynamic circular interaction between perceived problem and attempted solution can lead to an escalation of a problem situation (De Shazer, 1985; Watzlawick, Weakland and Fisch, 1974).

Common sense suggests the introduction of the 'opposite' as a solution in a problem situation. For example, if as a coach you notice that the athlete is depressed and lacks motivation you may go out of your way to cheer him up. Inadvertently, you may make him feel worse, pushing him deeper into apathy. Further, you may be taking the responsiblity of being his energiser. A pattern in the relationship may start developing where the athlete expects you to motivate activity in the training context or during competition.

While this may be necessary at times, it should not be rigidly ingrained in the relationship.

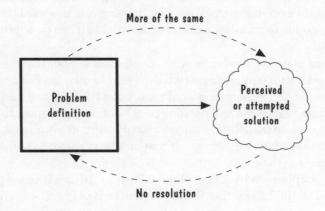

*Figure 16:  The problem definition 'boxes' you in, holding you hostage – only certain perceived solutions emerge*

Figure 16 refers to the circular connection between problem definition and perceived or attempted solution. Examine your assumptions of what you believe the problem to be. Constantly 'widen' and 'deepen' the initial problem definition. In the process, you will be creating other alternatives for action. Your definition of the problem may be what is boxing you in. This definition may be holding you hostage, not allowing the necessary freedom and creativity to introduce new complexity in your thinking.

Remember that the mind defines a problem to be a problem, when it is stuck and unable to resolve the situation it is encountering. It also defines the problem in such a way, that a solution becomes impossible if the old way of thinking is maintained. Otherwise, by definition, a problem cannot be defined as a problem. Resolution of a problem will always require something new or slightly different in your present restrictive thinking. My technique of using music to transcend obstacles (outlined in Chapter 5), is one way to bypass the restricted definition of what the mind believes the problem to be.

### Play with the Plan

Strategies are planned in mind. The map or plan is a static idea. The match however, takes place on a field; therefore, it is vital that the athlete is able to translate a coach's plan so that it can be applied on the field.

When planning strategies with athletes, remember that the map and the territory operate on two different levels. Do not assume that the players understand your plan, even though they may verbally state that they do. They may only be showing respect to you. Do not assume that players unconsciously support your map, even though they show agreement. It may not be possible to show disagreement in the group.

This explains why game plans fall apart during intense pressure, or in the interactive flow between two players or teams. A coach's map may therefore lose much of its value to the player as the match unfolds in complexity. The player may be suddenly confronted with demands and difficulties that your map may have been unable to predict. Remember that your plan is lifeless. It may exist in your mind. Parts of this plan may also exist in the players' minds. But it still can never incorporate all the complexity of a living match. A match unfolds and can never be fully predicted.

As a coach, you have no influence on the process that unfolds in the territory. This is extremely frustrating for a coach. You are actually powerless. All you can do is sit and watch as the players take on the responsibility of trying to put into practice that plan that had originated in your mind.

When presenting your plan to the players, create the opportunity for the players to connect the map to the demands that they encounter in their territory. The link between map and territory is provided by dialogue between coach and athlete. Two realities need to merge. This can be made possible by awareness and process coaching.

I often say to players 'let's play with the plan'. Athletes will start committing themselves to a coach's plan if they play around with the ideas in the plan. Players can be asked to speculate about 'what if' situations. What if the opposition played with three forwards and not the expected two forwards? How will this affect the plan?

What would my role be then? 'Playing with the plan' suggests that players verbally create possible problem situations. It also means that the players suggest suitable solutions. In the process, the players will be linking the plan with the demands of performing on the field.

## Let Us Talk

The relationship between the coach and athlete should ensure that constant dialogue allows for flow of ideas. Perspectives from both sides should be accepted – this provides for new information. New insights allow for further learning, thereby enhancing creativity in performance. If you do not have a coach, then a fellow athlete could help in providing you with an alternative perspective.

Bateson coined the term 'double description' to explain that extra depth (metaphorically) is obtained when the differences between two perceptions is integrated. When two individuals are able to produce meaningful news of difference for each other, then a new perspective of the situation is obtained. Bateson (1979: 76) termed this 'the difference that makes a difference'. The process creates more complexity and freedom in thinking.

In highly interactive team sports, such as rugby, football and hockey, participation in deciding on team strategy creates a powerful synergy in the group. As a coach, it is important to link each player's attainment of his individual goal in an interdependent manner. Different perspectives in the team need to be integrated into the whole.

The concept of shared responsiblity is introduced through the process of participation. Commitment to team is enhanced. Each individual reality needs to be listened to and accommodated. Each reality needs to be linked. It is recommended that players are divided into natural groups (for example, forwards, defenders, midfield), in order to converse and integrate differences into a meaningful whole. The coach can then connect these 'chunks' into the team plan. A meaningful map is being painted by the players. The coach needs to create the right context for this to occur. His responsibility is to integrate the flow into a synergetic whole.

## *We are in the Boat Together*

A fundamental principle of ecologic is that everything is connected to everything else. There is interdependence. Players are connected to each other. They are constantly influencing each other consciously and unconsciously. The nature of the relationships determines the complexity of the 'wholeness'. Unconscious resentments between members block energy flow. The section on energy flow in Chapter 3, should be continually borne in mind when trying to understand the development of synergetic wholeness.

On another level, this fundamental principle also implies that administrators, selectors, coaches, players, umpires/referees, spectators, media are connected and influence each other. The relationships that exist between these elements, influence actual performance on the field.

The interacting elements on a sports field are coaches, players and umpires/referees. As part of the wider perspective of wholeness of sporting performance in hockey, I introduced a mental training workshop for the hockey umpires. Interaction between players and umpires can become very stressful at times. Since umpires are in control of the unfolding process of interaction on the field, it is essential that they understand the nature of the interdependence between themselves and players. Umpires can escalate tension very quickly by the way they respond to the players. The opposite also applies. Some umpires are able to remain relaxed and calm, which then gets transmitted to the players.

A sporting system should carefully examine the nature of the connectedness between the interacting elements in the system. Although the team's performance is always visible on the field, the dynamic interaction of elements of players, coaches, selectors, administrators and media is never visible. However, these links can disrupt the energy flow of a team. Unconscious resentments between these subgroups can lower the team's performance and reduce the team's synergy. The improvement of performance on the field by a team is not only determined by coaching techniques. It is far more complex than this.

The relationship between administration and players is very important. Administrative issues and political infighting in committees will affect performance on the field. Clear boundaries need to exist between player and administrator levels. Excessive interference from administration about play will escalate tension and unhappiness with the players.

The demands of international sport are intense. The administrators will need to develop a clear, holistic vision of player development. Scientific and professional training programmes (physical, mental, tactical, technical) for the elite athlete groups together with developmental programmes to identify and then to select young athletes with the highest potential to reach the top are very important.

The decisions that administrators make will always affect the player. This was particularly evident in cricket and rugby. The decision to embark on the West Indies cricket tour (three one-day internationals, one full five-day international) with no warm-up matches, immediately after an intensive six-week World Cup tour created both physical and mental conditions which could not be met by skill or tactics. This type of decision creates difficulties and in the process undermines player confidence. Further, the sport in general may damage its image and take a two to three year knock in the eyes of the public.

With regard to international rugby, the two losses (against New Zealand and Australia) within a week generated a great deal of tension in all sections of the rugby family. The impossible was attempted on the field, and realistically, failure resulted. But what were the expectations? The media and public expectations and beliefs were 'frozen' in time. The point that I wish to make, is that conditions are created through administrative decisions that are often humanly impossible for players to cope with both physically and mentally (not withstanding tactically or technically).

I now wish to explore the connection between player and selector. Selectors have been entrusted with the responsibility of choosing players to represent a club, province or country. Selectors create their own policy, and focus on aspects of an athlete's play that are only known to each of the individual selectors. Selectors are only able to see play through their own individual eyes. Athletes therefore become 'dependent' on external recognition, via selection into a team. This may prove to be traumatic for athletes. A mismatch of inner beliefs about one's capabilities versus the external beliefs of an outsider may occur, generating resentment in the athlete.

The selection of the South African cricket team for the 1992 World Cup triggered country-wide emotionality. The dropping of Clive Rice (who captained the South African team to India in November 1991), Jimmy Cook and Peter Kirsten from the squad of 20 players, led to Clive Rice aggressively attacking the selectors in a television interview. While this behaviour cannot be condoned, it did highlight that certain players had felt cheated by the selectors. In particular, it was those players who had kept the game alive during those many years of isolation. Other interpersonal issues, other than playing ability, were being identified by the media as the reasons for the players being dropped. A nasty mess had developed. This conflict raises the question of whether players have a right to question selection decisions, or whether selectors 'owe' it to players to discuss the reasons for their selection decisions. The whole affair highlighted the emotional link that usually exists between players and selectors. A fundamental trust and respect must typify this link, otherwise resentment about 'unfair play' may enter the hearts of the players.

Selectors need to be aware of the interpersonal processes that they may unleash in a team due to their unwritten selection policies. Players need to feel that selectors have observed performance over time. Further, a policy of fairness and loyalty needs to be maintained. Rapid and continual changes of a team do not allow for holistic synergy to occur. In the 1974 rugby test match series against the British Lions, the South African team was not able to settle down and mould into a workable unit due to the high turnover of players. The performance on the field reflected individual isolated parts in motion.

Loyalty is a commodity that is not easily defined. With the constant moving of players between rugby provinces at present, loyalty will be severely tested. For the 1991 Currie Cup rugby final, the Transvaal selectors picked a player from another province who had not even played a club match in the Transvaal. On completion of the final, the player returned to his original province. Deep unconscious resentments may be unleashed in players that take a long time to heal. The players' loyalties and commitments on the field are linked to perceptions of the loyalty of the coach and selectors to the players. This is the dynamic link that exists between players and selectors.

Players need to understand that recognition may not arrive at a time when they feel it should. Likewise, being dropped may be unexpected and come as a shock. The unwritten code of sport implies that these events need to be handled with dignity. These are learning events that truly test the character of the sportsman. As South Africa returns to international competition, a number of experienced players may not gain selection. The timing may be just too late. Selection into a provincial or international team has to do with timing. Being in the right place, in the right position, at the right time is very much part of the quantum leap of selection.

The coach has a difficult position in the system. In some way, he will be expected to relate to all the interacting subgroups (administrators, selectors, media, players, umpires). The coach stands uniquely separate from these groups, yet always has to deal with external pressures being directed at him. He becomes the focus of responsibility. These pressures off the field far exceed the stresses of actually coaching the team.

The coach is connected to each of the players, as well as to the wholeness of the team. In team sports, the coach therefore needs to be working continually on two levels; the individual and the group. Although he is part of the team, he is distinctly separate from the team. He is the director of activities off the field, yet has no control on the field. He is always having to perform a balancing act when considering options. His most fundamental function, however, is to be aware of the pattern of interaction that exists in the team, both on and off the field. With this, he also needs to be aware of the pattern that exists between him and the team, and him and each of the individual players.

A team having interpersonal difficulty off the field, will show this difficulty in some way on the field. In other words, no distinction should be made between 'on' or 'off' the field. The synergy of a team is established off the field. The body language of players leaving the dressingroom, interpersonal space between players, and the manner of changeroom communication, are important indicators of the functioning of the team.

In the relationship between coach and athlete, information is constantly being exchanged on two levels. The task level and the relationship level. It is necessary for the coach to read feedback loops from the athlete about his ideas. As a coach, it is important to remember that your ideas are determined by your own mental structure of how and what you observe on the field. Keeney (1983: 80) states that 'one cannot separate the observer from the observed'. In other words, your ideas reflect more information about yourself, than what actually exists in 'reality'.

A clash of ideas between coach and athlete is therefore a clash of perception of reality. The coach should not force his own reality onto the athlete, or try and manipulate the athlete's reality so that it could fit better with his views. Instead, the evolution of a new reality needs to be created in conversation. The synergy that is created in this process provides the energy for outstanding performance.

A team develops a personality that is determined by the nature of the relationships between the players. There are teams that make one feel uncomfortable, where one cannot be oneself. There seem to be invisible restrictions on what one may say and how to behave. Other teams allow a freedom to respond with different ideas that enhance the individual value of each player. What is important to remember is that the nature of the relationships between players creates the ecosystem of the team. In addition, the nature of the relationships between team, coach, selectors and administrators also forms part of this ecosystem.

### Circles and Contradictions

When coaching, try and think in circles. Further, try and include yourself in the circle. For example, if you see an athlete failing at a particular task, ask yourself what circular processes may be occurring within the athlete and/or between you and the athlete.

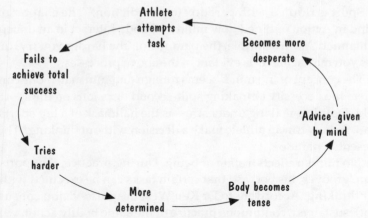

**Figure 17: Intrapersonal process that increases tension**
*The paradox of 'the harder you try, the less you achieve' is
evident in the circular process*

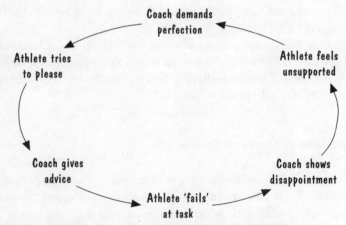

**Figure 18: Interpersonal process that increases tension**
*The success–failure circle of coach–athlete interaction*

The two processes outlined above interact with each other and
heighten the intrapersonal (internal) and interpersonal (coaching
relationship) stress of the athlete. As a coach, it is important to be
aware of these circular processes, and to intervene in such a way as
to break the escalating self-feeding nature of the circle.

Sport is riddled with paradox (contradiction). The chapter on Mind in Action outlined how mind and body interact in an unusual manner. As an example, the paradox of 'the harder you try, the less you may achieve' is evident in the above processes.

The concept of 'no mind' seems foreign and unusual, if one considers the necessity of making split-second decisions on the sports field. Decision-making under stress is the hallmark of a top sportsman. So how can an athlete make a decision without thinking? This presents a paradox.

'No mind' reflects a state of being. During practice, the sportsman 'grooves' his body so that certain tasks can be executed without thinking. According to Dr Ken West (a sports-vision consultant), sustained, continuous practise of the same bodily action will result in muscle memory (West, Calder and Bressan, 1992). As the body operates in space, and clicks into the groove, the mind does not need to think. It is like walking. You do not have to think of how to walk. The paradox is if you try and think and analyse how to take each step while walking, you will find that your flow and rhythm of walking will be affected.

Complex bodily actions are beyond the analytical understanding of the mind. The mind, however, needs to understand how the body learns best. Paradoxically, the body operates best without the interference and help of the mind.

### Experiences in Time and Space

Experiences of time and space are influenced by the interpersonal context in which you are involved. As an example, ask players from opposing sides of their experiences of time during a soccer or hockey match with the score at 1-0 and five minutes left to play. The players in the winning team may express how slowly the time passed, especially if they were holding onto the result under tremendous pressure from the opposition. Players from the losing side will generally feel that the time disappeared quickly and that if they had some extra time they would have scored.

It is important for the coach to understand that the experience of time and the concept of space is uniquely subjective, depending on the context that an athlete finds himself in. Each athlete experiences unique demands in space and time that cannot be totally understood by the coach.

In individual time-focus sports, such as athletics and swimming, the experience of time is not objective. I have become acutely aware of this phenomenon during the process of writing. There are days when time disappears. I lose myself, unaware of what my watch is actually telling me. Actual hours, as reflected by my watch, feel like minutes. I am unable to compare time frames across days. The experience of time is determined by the context that you are operating in and in your ability to enter into and become one with the moment.

It is necessary for athletes and swimmers to experience time in a variety of contexts. Sitting quietly, repeatedly counting from one to ten for two minutes feels different from swimming the 200 metre butterfly in which you are attempting to break the two minute record. When consulting with athletes who are attempting to break a time record or set up a personal best, I enquire what the time barrier is. With them sitting quietly, I start the stop watch and ask them to tell me when they think that that magical time has been reached. This experience allows them freedom to explore time without the restriction of the mind creating a self-imposed time barrier.

The four-minute mile provided a tremendous psychological barrier to athletes, until Roger Bannister achieved the impossible. The mind creates time barriers that are linked to a context. Instead of the mind being trapped by time as being a magical four minutes, athletes could have transformed this barrier to be 240 seconds. The mind perceives a significant difference in meaning between four minutes and three minutes 59 seconds (this presents a change of one whole minute if you focus on the minute level). However, the difference between 240 and 239 seconds only represents a change of one second. In actual 'clock' time there is no difference.

In mark-down sales, for example, articles can change in price from R10 to R9.99. Our minds often interpret this as being a one rand drop (on the rand level), while in actual fact it is only a one cent drop. When shopping the next time, notice how many articles are at the something-rand-99-cents level. A one cent increase may in fact make the article too expensive, due to the jump on the rand level.

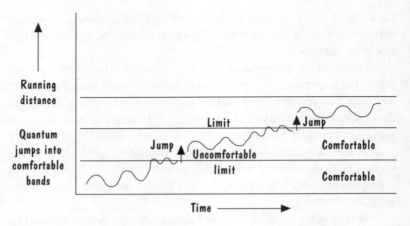

*Figure 19:   Comfortable bands and uncomfortable 'limits'*

In long distance and marathon running the perception of distance may vary. Figure 19 reflects the distance limits that both mind and body may experience. This is particularly true for novices who have decided to take up marathon running. An interaction between what is uncomfortable in both mind and body occurs as new limits are approached and then conquered.

During running, both your mind and body become familiar with the demands of a certain level. As you operate on this plateau there is relative ease of action. The mind and body are able to adapt quickly. You will start realising that your own expectations of yourself become the limit to how far your body will go. As you touch new limits you will experience discomfort in both mind and body. This may prove to be exhausting. However, it is necessary to break through mind barriers regarding distance to be run. Do not rush this process and push ahead regardless. Breaking through a limit is a critical time, when most physical injuries are likely to occur.

Novice runners should be careful of doing too much, too soon, too quickly. Being able to run longer distances than previously covered, takes time. Beware of over-extension. There should be a delicate balance between the comfortable and the uncomfortable; in the beginning, it is better to err on the side of caution and comfortableness in body.

With time, the mind and body will find a new equilibrium. Distances that previously felt long, can now be covered without the mind worrying about the actual distance. Instead, the mind starts relaxing and losing itself, as the body unthinkingly journeys. Mind and body oneness occurs. Distance becomes irrelevant. If you drop to a lower level, feel the ease at which both your mind and body experience a shorter distance. Distance becomes relatively subjective.

## THE PSYCHOLOGY OF COACHING STYLES

I now want to examine two concepts of coaching style that fit with systemic thinking, namely 'shared responsibility' and 'awareness and process coaching'. In order to use these ideas, it will be necessary for you to give up some of the control that you believe you have in organising the athlete, and to trust in the athlete's learning ability. In other words, this style of coaching may initially create uncertainty and doubt within yourself. It is worth mentioning that these feelings are normal, since you may be confronting old comfortable beliefs.

For an athlete, the two important ingredients for successful learning in sport, are being aware of the interactive flow (in body and in mind) of what he does on the field; and to assume as much responsibility for his own meaningful development (physical and mental) as possible. The coach should help the athlete to learn more about himself during performance, as well as in the build-up to an important match.

### Shared Responsibility – A Journey of Togetherness

I believe that coaches take on too much responsibility in trying to develop athletes. They even try and take on the responsibility of thinking and planning for the athlete. I contend that coaches give too much. They always want to help.

There is a belief that the coach knows best. 'Good' coaching will therefore require instruction and advice. It is assumed that if the athlete follows the advice, then matches will be won and records broken. A relationship is being established where a coach 'tells' and the athlete is expected to 'follow' the instructions. A coaching pattern starts developing.

I experienced this pattern in a mental training session with the South African under-21 hockey team. The players walked into the room expecting to be activated by me. They were passively expecting me to give them something. I just sat. I waited. In the process, a great deal of uneasiness was built up. What now? I posed the question: 'What do you want to talk about?' This was an unexpected question, since it clashed with their expectation that 'We have come to get advice from an expert'. The process of trying to redefine the expectations in the mental training context was hard going. We were struggling to redefine the rules of the coaching relationship. At the end of the session, one player remarked: 'Does this mean that we should become our own psychologist?' Yes, in a sense it means exactly that.

During his extensive training, Brian Mitchell told his trainers exactly what he thought. He actively assumed responsibility for his own development. 'I told them how I felt on the road runs, and that I now needed a bit of speed work. Must start cutting down, no sparring to-day.' Taking on this responsibility led to his success. He did not use it to get out of hard training. Instead, his in-depth knowledge of his body limits, and his own personal training requirements ensured that he was fully prepared for his fights. Of fundamental importance in this process, is honesty with yourself. Brian emphasised this point. There are no easy short cuts.

Each player needs to be taught to take on the responsibility of developing himself. What needs to happen, is to determine what the player believes he needs to develop. This can be elicited in conversation with the coach. 'What are your concerns?', 'How can I assist you?', 'What is meaningful for you at this moment?' Note that the coach poses questions. Creating the context for this dialogue is the responsibilty of the coach. In the discussion, a player's reality is being challenged in a meaningful manner. Further, the coach becomes aware of how the player is actually perceiving himself and his difficulties on the field. The coach gets the picture from the player. The coach never makes assumptions. The coach provides the canvas, paints and brushes. The player paints. The coach observes. The coach may want to add a few strokes of the brush to 'brighten', or 'soften', or 'colour', or 'detail a specific', in the player's picture. This is not forced. Be careful of prescription. Instead, a picture is a personal item. It needs to be respected. In the process, the player learns to become his own psychologist, his own physical trainer, his own coaching strategist, his own dietician, his own monitor. He is taking on the responsibility for his own development in a holistic way.

In team sports, players can start coaching and developing each other. They can also monitor the progress that is being made. As an example, ask each player what he feels he needs to develop in his play. You will notice that the skills that each player wishes to develop are cybernetically linked. There are opposites which can be meaningfully connected. For example, in a hockey team, one player may want to improve his tackling while another may wish to learn to beat a defender. Link these. The goalkeeper may wish to improve his sliding out of goal, while a forward may want to improve his calmness when approaching the goal. Link these. Each player should now monitor the progress of self and the other player during practice. Information from the two different perspectives will provide meaningful insights. Both players are working simultaneously on their own problems as well as helping to solve the difficulties of the other. In the process, meaningful connections are being forged naturally.

A coach should always examine his own ideas about what he thinks a player or team needs to develop. Athletes are often taken through meaningless, alienating exercises. The relationship between coach and athlete is a difficult one. Players often act stupid, and force the coach to take on the responsibilty of directing activity. When the coach takes the lead in deciding what should be done, the players unconsciously start dragging their feet and feel uncommitted.

A coach's responsibility is to create an interpersonal context where players take on responsibility for their own development. This enhances learning. Involvement and commitment is increased. Meaningful insights are obtained. The concept of shared responsibility is based on participation in the process. As a coach, you may feel that you are not doing your job if you decide to adopt the position that I am suggesting. This is a real feeling that is telling you something important about yourself. Reflect on this, as was suggested in the previous chapter in the section on the sporting koan. Coaching teaches you more about yourself than it teaches actual skills to players.

## Awareness and Interaction Coaching

I believe that coaches talk too much. Instructions are easy to give. While the mind may understand, words are not understood by the body. The body operates in space, moving in action. Verbal and nonverbal information operate on two different levels. It is imperative that the coach connects mind and body. This can be achieved through awareness coaching.

As a coach, the one side of the coin of awareness coaching is awareness of self. In order to implement awareness coaching, the coach needs to be fully aware of himself in interaction with players: his feelings, the way he speaks, his impact on others, and the environment in which he is operating. The other side of the coin of awareness coaching is getting the athlete to understand the 'messages' that his body is giving him. The work of Gallwey (1976, 1986) provides tremendous insight into how a coach can develop an athlete's body awareness in performance.

There is a fundamental difference in the type of language a coach uses, when comparing traditional instruction coaching and awareness coaching. A generalised distinction is that information is given, and instructions conveyed in traditional coaching, whereas in awareness coaching, questions are posed by the coach that direct the player's mind to the feel in body. In other words, questions that link the mind to the body. The questions posed can then guide the inner process of learning in the athlete.

In *The Inner Game of Golf*, Gallwey outlines a process that increases awareness in putting. The focus can be on awareness of putter head speed, direction of path of the putter head, length of swing, angle of the club's face before and after contact. In the execution of a putt, a golfer feels a certain sensation in the body. On locating the specific feel in the specific part of the body, the golfer focuses his mind on the body sensation. In the process, the golfer heightens his awareness of how the body feels while executing a stroke. Slight differences in body feel during the stroke, will result in differences of actual execution. To heighten the feel even further, Gallwey suggests that the golfer closes his eyes while putting. Throughout performance, the golfer focuses his mind on body sensation during the playing of the shot. The body starts telling the mind when things are not working. In addition, the body will have the ability to self-correct since it becomes aware of the 'right' feel as compared to the 'wrong' feel.

In any problem situation that may occur on the field, ask the player what he noticed. Who was close to him? What were his feelings? How did he try and solve the difficulty in the moment? Standing here talking, how would he have responded differently looking back? What does he feel he still needs to develop in order to improve? Notice that all these questions are not 'why' questions, which tend to imply judgement, as well as leading to theorising and speculation. What, how, when, who questions connects the player to the interactive process on the field. This is process coaching. These questions heighten player awareness, and stimulate the player's own problem solving ability.

Interpersonal connections can be made in a team sport, if the coach asks other players if they had noticed what was happening to this specific player? How did it affect them? What did they do about the difficulty? This process builds up a maze of meaningful connections between players. An awareness of interdependence is highlighted.

The process in awareness coaching allows the player the opportunity to create his own meaningful reality. This reality can be shaped through the types of questions asked. The coach should endeavour to get the player to make his own connections in how the difficulty may have started. The reality of this problem should include those actions of his which contributed to the difficulty, and should also incorporate methods to improve the situation, highlighting skills development in practice.

Awareness coaching is linked to process coaching. There is no beginning. There is no end. Players and coach are on a journey. The coach's responsibility is to enhance learning.

## A UNIQUE EXPERIENCE – CO-OPERATIVE COMPETITIVENESS

The South African Men's Hockey Association (known as South African Hockey Association since unification), developed a unique programme of tactical, technical, physical, vision skills and mental training under the guidance of Jock Coombes, the ex-Director of Coaching. The fundamental philosophy of the programme is to develop players and coaches in a meaningful way based on systemic and integrative principles.

Since 1990, a number of courses on mental training have been conducted for the provincial and national coaches. The objective is to create a context of learning where old traditional styles of coaching are challenged. Old beliefs and rigid thinking are discussed. In the process, concepts such as 'shared responsibilty' and 'awareness coaching' are covered. The idea is for coaches to think about their own thinking, since coaches are responsible for developing a healthy functioning team.

'Conversation of ideas', with both/and options to any issue is a valued norm. Relevant issues need to be discussed openly. As an example, 'What does a coach do with a highly talented flair player who does not want to conform to the group?' This issue does not have a simple answer. In fact, I find it extremely difficult to even venture an 'expert' comment on this particular difficulty. What emerges in the shared context of discussion, however, allows for creative insights for all the coaches. This would never have been possible without shared participation.

The philosophy of co-operative sharing does not clash with competitiveness on the field. In fact, it has been noticed that the competitiveness has increased, with players performing at very high standards. Gallwey (1976:111) offers us the reason:

> 'So we arrive at the startling conclusion that true competition is identical with true cooperation. Each player tries his hardest to defeat the other, but in this use of competition it isn't the other person we are defeating; it is simply a matter of overcoming the obstacles he presents. In true competition no person is defeated. Both players benefit by the efforts to overcome the obstacles presented by the other. Like two bulls butting their heads against one another, both grow stronger and each participates in the development of the other.'

During the 1991 interprovincial tournament, a consultation team was established in order to assist coaches and players during the intensive week of hockey. Horst Wein (highly respected ex-German international player), Jock Coombes and myself formed the consultation team. The consultation team was a service for the coaches (primarily) and players. In particular, the service offered tactical and technical advice and guidance, as well as ideas concerning the mental preparation of teams. 'No force and prescription' was the one value that we as consultants held foremost.

Coaches were given the opportunity to define the nature of the assistance that they believed that was needed. In the process, the opinions and ideas of the coaches needed to be respected. We, as consultants, believed that the coaches knew best when it came to the 'help' that they were seeking for their respective teams. Of the 12 provincial teams at the tournament, only one team did not seek assistance in the mental preparation of the players. This was respected. The fact that 11 teams were prepared to share the same sports psychologist is unique.

Coaches and teams normally want to 'own' the sports psychologist. This is a very real issue that needs careful consideration. The sports psychologist is viewed by coaches as an extremely valuable tool to increase the chances of winning. In working with a team, the psychologist starts identifying with the culture of the team, he feels the inner excitement of the players as the big match approaches. He plans strategies on a mental level with the players. The objective is to enhance performance. The objective is to help the team win. This is a normal process that a sports psychologist must undergo while working with a team or athlete. An identification with the team is normal.

Having said this, I believe that 'ownership' of the sports psychologist may reduce his effectiveness. I believe that the sports psychologist should always have the improvement of healthy sports attitudes of all players as the core of his philosophy. Sport, in general, is his focus. During my work with the 11 provincial teams at the tournament, I was amazed at the diversity of issues that each team was encountering. A team is a living organism. Each team has its own personality. At the tournament, I was dealing with 11 different personalities.

My philosophy was that if each team was able to transcend some of the difficulties that were being encountered, then hockey as a sport would benefit. More creative energy from each of the sides would be available for actual on-the-field performance. This proved to be the case. Absolutely no competitive edge was lost in the process.

It is often difficult to gauge the impact of involvement with coaches and/or teams if the team has not won (using score as the criteria). However, at the end of the tournament some interesting comments were made by the coaches that highlighted some of the meaning of the week's experience: 'I have never felt more relaxed at a tournament.' 'It was interesting to get diverse views on how complex coaching really is.' 'It was nice to know that there was always somebody to talk to – coaching can become very lonely.' 'I valued the support and opportunity to bounce off my ideas.'

The main aim was to establish a support system where ideas can be shared in a non-threatening way. The interprovincial hockey week in Durban, 1991, was unique. It was an experience where the focus went beyond winning.

As we enter the era of establishing the nature of the new South Africa, national bodies of the various sports need to consider creating a context where provincial coaches can come together to share ideas. Coaching issues need to be explored from different perspectives. Mental training workshops should be offered to the coaches in order to develop their skills. A norm of co-operative dialogue will allow for creative newness in problem solving. In the process, the national team will emerge with more synergetic power.

## VALUE SYSTEMS AND MOTIVATION

As more and more cultural integration occurs in our country, our provincial and national teams will have to incorporate a range of individual differences. There is tremendous diversity of value systems operating in the South African context at any given time. This diversity needs to be understood and utilised, without imposing a homogeneity. A South African sporting team is likely to reflect a range of differences in values.

The new flavour of our national teams will be rich in cultural complexity. This is exciting. In the apartheid era, our national teams were mostly white. Facilities were inadequate in the communities of our other population groups and this tended to hinder the progress of athletes in these communities. Times have now changed. For example, our national marathon runners are all black, while the national soccer team is predominantly black. Our national teams are developing a new type of personality that all our people can support and identify with.

South Africa has entered the multi-cultural era. I believe that cultural or racial differences trap your perceptions. There is presently a great fad in multi-cultural everythings that are doing their rounds in South Africa; multi-cultural education, multi-cultural counselling, multi-cultural negotiation and so on. This is restrictive thinking. In sport, coaches will need to think about individual differences in their teams in a way that transcends 'multi-cultural'. Dr Don Beck and Christopher Cowan of The National Values Center in Texas offer the coach of any team exciting insights in the differences of value systems of individuals, irrespective of skin colour.

This model contends that different cultures have evolved through patterns of thinking over time. The focus is on understanding how the challenges and problems in any interpersonal context, have created ways of thinking to deal with the demands of the given situation. An evolutionary spiral of complexity in thinking emerges over time depending on the contextual conditions operating at that given time.

> 'Crucibles (problems of existence) forge new solutions (paradigms) for the new problems. In time the New Order will run into difficulty because as it solves problems it creates new ones. Then a new crucible is reached and, once again, a fresh paradigm is formed to address those emerging problems. Such a process has continued throughout history.' (Beck and Linscott, 1991: 32)

According to Beck and Linscott, eight value systems of thinking have emerged. They have evolved in complexity to form a spiral. The 'pattern of thinking' that presents itself depends on the conditions of existence an individual finds himself in.

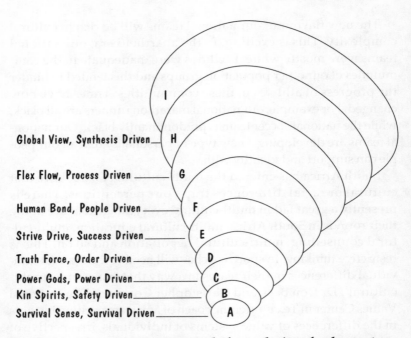

Global View, Synthesis Driven — H

Flex Flow, Process Driven — G

Human Bond, People Driven — F

Strive Drive, Success Driven — E

Truth Force, Order Driven — D

Power Gods, Power Driven — C

Kin Spirits, Safety Driven — B

Survival Sense, Survival Driven — A

*Figure 20: The evolutionary spiral of complexity of value systems*
Reprinted with special permission of Dr Don Beck, The National
Values Center, Denton, Texas, USA

These patterns of thinking are neither good or bad. They were
appropriate for the existential difficulties that were being confronted. They should therefore not be judged. In the Beige A level of
thinking, the individual is survival driven. In the Purple B level,
the individual is safety driven. The Red C level is power driven,
while the Blue D level is order driven. In the Orange E level, the
person is success driven. The individual in the Green F level is people driven. The person in the Yellow G and Turquoise H levels is
process and synthesis driven. These levels form the human evolutionary spiral.

Thinking levels can 'drop' to a lower level if existential conditions change. However, higher level thinking evolves over time.
You cannot be before your time. Through one's own development
and learning (formal and informal), the mind's way of thinking is
able to make a quantum leap to the next level. This process in not

| World Conditions/ Problems of Existence | Appropriate Coping System |
|---|---|
| A: a state of nature | act much like other animals |
| B: mysterious and frightening | placate spirits, join together for safety |
| C: rough and hard like a jungle | fight to survive in spite of others |
| D: divinely controlled and guilt driven | obey rightful higher authority |
| E: full of viable alternatives | pragmatically test options for success |
| F: the habitat of all humanity | join communities to experience growth |
| G: in danger of collapse | stand alone to learn to be free |
| H: a single living entity | seek the order beneath the Earth's chaos |

time driven in the sense that a person has to spend a year in one level in order to pass into the next (as is the case at formal school).

Each individual's thinking pattern and world view will fall into one of these value systems. For an individual, different value systems may apply in different contexts. Or, different value systems may reveal themselves in the same context over time. Although an individual's thinking should evolve over time, it may become trapped in a rigid mind-set and remain at a particular level.

In any team, individuals are likely to vary in their respective value systems. A team's wholeness may be disrupted if there is a clash between the value systems of the individual players. For example, player X operating from within the Red C level may be individualistic and egocentric in his play, which in turn affects the discipline of the team. Player Y, who is order driven, and obedient in following a game plan, may resent the irresponsible individualistic action of player X. As potential conflict heightens, player Z, who is success driven and sets goals to achieve, may become disillusioned since both he and the team are not progressing and winning. Player W, who is a humanitarian operating within the Green F level, may try and seek consensus and equality in the team. In trying to get players X, Y, and Z to tolerate and accept each other, he may inadvertently cause more conflict since these players may feel that player W has no right to interfere. A series of destructive processes may be unleashed in the team, as the value systems of individual players clash. The coach is also operating from a particular value system level, which will determine the way he perceives the interactions in the team, and the way in which he will intervene when trying to resolve the difficulties.

An application of Beck and Linscott's model to the mode of motivation by coaches is outlined:

| Thinking Pattern | Mode of Motivation of Coach |
| --- | --- |
| Red – Power base system | appeals to the inner drive of force and power – 'might is right' |
| Blue – Truth force | authority and discipline – 'one right way' |
| Orange – Ambition to improve | sets goals for achievement strategic and analytical – 'get ahead' |
| Green – Human harmony | humanistic, warm, caring interpersonal relationships – 'equality of everyone' |

A coach should never believe that individual athletes think in the same way as he does. A coach operating from a systemic perspective will incorporate the healthy elements of thinking from all of these value systems: survival needs; ritual and tradition; strong competitive self-image; discipline and commitment; desire to improve to be the best; emotional warmth and affiliation; competency and freedom of choice; creative problem solving; holistic and integrative thinking; evolutionary development; are all concerns of the systemic thinker. Integrating these values into a team's thinking promotes a creative and synergetic whole that is able to make a quantum leap in performance. Further, the systemic thinking coach will be able to connect with the players and the team in an appropriate manner, depending on the needs of the team, and the situation the team finds itself in.

In essence, the systemic coach will be able to utilise the values from one motivational mode, depending on the needs of the group at a given time. Autocratic discipline, for example, may be necessary. Without discipline and structure, a team is likely to fragment under pressure. Dedication combined with a disciplined work ethic is an ingredient for sporting success. Setting goals with players and striving to achieve success taps the values in the Orange value system, where achievement and success are driving forces. Allowing democratic decisions at times, with evidence of emotional support and caring, further ensures a high level of synergy in the team.

Motivation is a misunderstood phenomenon. In order to activate inner meaning for any athlete, the coach may need to incorporate multi-levelled motivational messages that tap one or more of the value systems. The systemic coach has his focus on the diversity of value systems that may emerge in a team. Further, the systemic coach knows that his team has to incorporate all these value systems in order for healthy functioning to occur.

## CHAPTER 5
# Be prepared – no intensity!

At present, there is tremendous interest in the field of sports psychology in South Africa. Coaches and athletes are becoming more aware of the benefits of a thorough mental training programme. The media's exposure of my involvement with the Natal rugby team in the 1990 Currie Cup final, provided a forum for discussion of the type of mental techniques that could enhance performance. Suddenly coaches were seeking the golden key to get their team to win. Motivation was the catch word being tossed around in conversation.

Oneness (or mind/body integration) in performance is the ultimate goal for the athlete. This is like a high, a form of enlightenment. Before this can be achieved, however, the athlete must first become aware of the contradictory, and at times, disruptive nature of the interfering mind in stressful situations. Further, oneness in the team is most likely to be achieved, when individual goals and energies are juxtaposed. A new synergetic level is then reached.

Elite athletes have to deal with stress. Being able to perform under pressure will be expected. I will therefore be looking at stress and relaxation in more depth. More specifically, I will be examining the effects of heightened stress on performance. Debilitating stress, however, should not be confused with proper arousal for action.

In accordance with the concept of dynamic balance, relaxation is necessary in order to be creatively aroused and to ensure spontaneous energy flow in performance. I will therefore be exploring ideas about relaxed and focused performance.

Top athletes are mentally tough. This concept is often misunderstood. I therefore found it necessary to look at mental toughness more closely. I was fortunate to explore ideas in my interviews with some of our elite sportsmen.

I have been busy researching new ways to enhance performance. In particular, new techniques have been developed through my sports consultancy, MIND IN SPORT. I intend exploring the techniques of using music and imagery to enhance performance.

### Time for Calmness and Clearness

1992 has been the year of re-entry to international sport. I always believed that the mental preparation of our elite sportsmen has lagged significantly behind physical, tactical and skills training. However, the recent cricket, rugby, soccer, and Olympic results have shown that all aspects of our training and coaching methods need to be carefully examined. Years of isolation have stunted our growth. It seems that we have stopped thinking. We have been caught in a time warp.

Now is the time for calmness and careful evaluation of the present situation that sport finds itself in. A mental map is needed to plan and direct our thinking for the future. Changes will take time. Our advantage is that we are starting out a fresh.

'The universe is sacred.
You cannot improve it.
If you try to change it, you will ruin it.
If you try to hold it, you will lose it.' (Page, 1989:60, Verse 29)

The value of 'not knowing' allows for a freedom to be, without the mind restricting action. In a sense this presents the picture of the unspoilt beauty of a child or the untouched beauty of a natural ecosystem or rain forest. There is no pollution.

We are at the bottom. It was only our own expectations that were being built up over these years of loneliness, that had created the belief that we were champions. Maybe these expectations had offered us security.

In our planning, mistakes that have been made in other countries should be avoided. Methods that have proved successful for other cultural contexts need adaptation to suit our unique conditions. Success will depend on whether we are able to start healthy processes of learning in our own sporting contexts.

Man's 'helpful' intervention into any situation may inadvertently create difficulties on some level. The issue of the amount of mental preparation and the role of the sports psychologist is a point at hand. In the early 1970's mental preparation was very fashionable in American gridiron football. Every team had its own resident sports psychologist. The coach and sports psychologist had to define special roles for each other so that nobody stood on each other's toes. As time went on, a re-assessment was needed. The players were being made more tense by all the demands that were being made on them (including mental training). The players were becoming mental about mental training. This is a very real issue that psychologists, coaches and players need to be aware of. The belief that 'if a little of something' works, then 'more of that something' will work better is an erroneous assumption.

As stated previously, the fundamental concept of dynamic balance needs to apply in any situation. Too much of anything never works. This is going against the law of nature. Be careful of maximising. At present, there are now only a handful of American gridiron teams with full-time sports psychologists. Instead, sports psychologists are now being consulted when necessary, depending on the needs of the coach and players.

There are three main interacting roles that need to be considered when looking at mental preparation: the athlete, the coach, and the psychologist. Of these, the psychologist is the outsider, a position that needs to be maintained because a neutral, balanced perspective is the outsider's strength.

There is a real need for proper mental training of our elite sportsmen. As we become more and more involved in international competition, that need for proper mental training will increase. The issue is to decide on the format and the timing of the mental training programme. Proper timing of any input or intervention will allow for meaningful impact. The unique format of the programme needs to be conjointly developed with the coach and discussed with the players. The success of mental preparation is largely determined by the inner urgency and desire of the athlete to improve his own mental attitude.

It is worth mentioning at this point that the Natal rugby team had reached the 1990 Currie Cup final without any formal mental

training by a psychologist. Ian McIntosh, the coach, had developed
the players through his own efforts. The relationships that were
evident in the team had been moulded by him. My involvement
with the team was of short duration – three sessions of two hours in
the evenings leading up to the Currie Cup final. I was not involved
with the team on the actual day. There was no formal relaxation, no
visualisation, no goal setting on the match day. I believed that any
involvement on my part on that day would have interfered with
the natural healthy functioning of the team. The team had to trust
in their own abilities.

## THE COACH — DIRECTOR OF OPERATIONS

As the coach, you are the central cog of the system. The coach sets
the tone in a team. Unknowingly a culture is created by the coach:
interpersonal values are established during the coaching process;
relationships are forged. The demands on coaches are increasing.
As sport develops to new heights, the coach is under pressure to
gain new techniques and improve his knowledge. He has to keep
abreast of the latest ideas in areas such as physiotherapy, psychology, technique and tactics, diet and training methods. Elementary
training courses in these fields need to be given to enhance the
skills of the coach.

A coach is also like a surrogate parent to the players. Coaching is
complex. The demands on the coach are enormous. With provincial and international teams, the coach also has to deal with the
media. When a team is not winning, sponsorships may be with-
drawn. Expectations of the supporters can fuel further pressure on
the coach. He becomes the focus of attention, and has to deal with
his own inner stress levels.

As coach and athlete/team evolve together over time, there will
be a number of ups and downs to deal with. This is the rhythm of
sport. As the coach interacts with the team, he may become aware
that the functioning of the team is not up to standard: performance
of individuals may be below potential; there seems to be a block
somewhere. The coach may be unable to solve these difficulties – in
fact, the problem may not be easily defined. In the process, perfor-

mance may worsen. At this point, the coach may believe that the players need a motivator to energise them to perform better.

Alternatively, the players may be approaching an important tournament or match. Careful preparation on all levels is needed. Mental preparation becomes part of this build-up. This preparation becomes more complex during a World Cup tournament that spans four weeks, or the two weeks of the Olympics. National coaches are having to deal with the complexity of energy flow of players over time (refer to Chapter 3). Timing of arousal, periods of relaxation, dealing with prolonged periods of stress, are only some of the concerns of the coach. The trend for most international teams is to have a management team consisting of a team manager, coach, assistant coach, physiotherapist, medical doctor, psychologist and dietician. Some of these positions can be on a consultative basis. The role of the psychologist needs to be carefully defined. The relationship between coach and psychologist is an extremely important link.

These present the two situations that most warrant the introduction of a psychologist: firstly, to resolve a difficulty in the team that may be hindering performance on the field, and secondly, to help prepare athletes for the mental demands of international competition, or to prepare a team/athlete for peak performance for an important match or final. If the desire to use the psychologist is driven by an obsessional need to win, then you as coach are unconsciously going against the laws of nature. The desperation to win may then in fact be the problem that needs to be dealt with, before the athlete can feel free and relaxed to perform.

The opposite may also apply. As a coach, you may never want the intrusion of an outsider. This may be seen as a threat. No interference is safe. Although this should be respected, this belief may be the very problem that you need to deal with. You may be smothering the players and not allowing new complexity of thinking. Therefore always examine why you feel that a psychologist or outside motivator should be consulted. Or why you feel that you may be against the introduction of an outside consultant, despite the fact that the players may have expressed a need for outside help.

I believe that a coach, operating from an ecosystemic philosophy (as outlined in Chapter 4), is most able to create a healthy team that incorporates and integrates player diversity, and values active player participation in discussion of problem situations. It is worth repeating that this philosophy will always offer alternatives in problem-solving as long as you focus on the interconnectedness of the players. Each player can provide a meaningful insight into a problem situation if he is given the space to present his reality.

## THE NEEDS OF THE ATHLETE

The athlete should always have a basic mental training programme. Areas such as goal-setting, periods of relaxation for visualisation, gaining insight into some of your strengths and weaknesses as a player are important aspects of mental preparation. As a player, you need to take on the responsibility of your own progress in this field. This mental training can be planned with the coach, or another athlete who is respected. Discussion with a sports psychologist may also prove to be useful. It is important to find the format that feels comfortable for you.

In my discussions with Brian Mitchell, Bruce Fordyce, Jonty Rhodes and Jimmy Cook, it became clear that they all took full responsibility for their own mental preparation. This occurred in a spontaneous and natural way. Bruce stated that he did informal visualisation of the Comrades route during his training runs. Tough hills are rehearsed in his mind. Strategies of when to pass opponents are spontaneously planned in his mind while out training. Further, Bruce has a theme song or piece of music that is able to arouse him to suitable levels of training performance. In the process, Bruce is getting mentally ready for the big day.

Brian Mitchell used to have a ritual training programme before each of his world title fights. Ten days before the fight, he would put himself through a physically and mentally taxing gym fight. He had to put himself through severe stress and pressure in order to see how he coped with the situation.

According to Jonty Rhodes, he does not have a formal mental preparation programme. Having said this, I feel that this should not be misunderstood. Jonty tries to leave his planning and mental preparation for as late as possible. 'Too much thinking makes me tense,' he says. This is an extremely significant comment. Jonty has come to understand that the waiting phase should not be filled with too much thought on what is likely to happen in the match. Too much intense planning and preparation may create rigid mind-sets, as well as activate unnecessary psychic and physical energy.

There should be an inner desire to gain more understanding of yourself in performance, a need for self-improvement. Part of gaining more insight into your performance is done by discussing some of your difficulties with a neutral third party, like a psychologist. Experience with a sports psychologist should involve 'conversation of ideas'. By this I mean that you should not expect external motivation from the psychologist. The process is more complex. You should be driven by an internal desire to gain a new perspective of yourself and your performance during the discussion. In addition, you will need to take on the responsibility of then implementing some of the ideas that may have emerged during the discussion.

There may be times when you lack motivation. Your performance may have declined. The love for the game may also have diminished. This could be due to a number of factors. The possible reasons for a drop in performance need to be explored, and a plan of action needs to be mapped out in discussion.

There may be times when you may have been forced to consult with a psychologist. Your coach may believe that you need to improve your mental toughness. If you are not inwardly happy to discuss some of your difficulties with an outsider, you may develop an inner resistance. If there is an inner resentment or a belief that a 'shrink' cannot be trusted, do not be surprised if the input is meaningless. Expectations always shape behaviour.

I do believe that elite sportsmen are continually operating under stressful pressures. This is the nature of modern sport. The mind can become trapped in the process. Internal conflicts and doubts may emerge. Further, downward spirals of performance may be mismanaged by the athlete. Difficulties in the relationship with the coach may emerge. The manifestations of all of these will be a decline in performance. A sports psychologist can be of assistance in helping the athlete gain better understanding of his difficulties. Obstacles can be removed, so that creative energy can be released. A freedom of mind should result after consultation with a sports psychologist.

## INDIVIDUAL AND TEAM

The table below gives a brief outline of some of the important aspects of mental preparation that both individual and team need to consider. It is important to emphasise that the individual and team levels are continually interacting with one another.

| INDIVIDUAL | TEAM |
| --- | --- |
| Visualisation and Imagery | Relationships |
| Focus and Flow | Problem Solving |
| Critical Moments in Match | Emotional Support |
| Relaxation | Communication |
| Awareness Levels | Creating a Powerful Whole |
| Setting Goals | Directed Synergy |
| Dealing with Stress | Healthy Team Functioning |
| Knowing Strengths/Weaknesses | Discipline |

The link between individual and team level is extremely important. Individual and team goals need to be integrated. Energies need to be focused in a direction, with committed purpose.

In Chapters 1 and 2, I covered the individual aspects of mental training, while in Chapters 3 and 4, the focus was on the interactive flow of activity and the development of team synergy.

On an individual player level, it is necessary to focus on the mind and body interaction; while on the team level, it is important to focus on the interaction of different minds that make up the group.

## DEALING WITH STRESS

Sportsmen must be able to monitor, direct, release and utilise stressful energy. An individual and team evolves and changes over time. A team is a living organism.

Peak performance is dependent on how one gathers energy in the build-up to an event. Energy is the vital commodity. Without it, there is no activity. Remember that an individual and team flow in upward and downward cycles over time. Careful monitoring of energy flow needs to occur. Old tensions need to be released at the right time in order to allow for regeneration of new energy.

A World Cup competition or an Olympics adds further complexity in dealing with stress build-up. Athletes living together over a time period will generate additional tension, unlike the case of a one-off match or event.

Athletes have to deal with two levels of stress. Firstly, there is the stress build-up, as the important match draws nearer; secondly, there are the stresses of the actual match that can surface during performance.

### *Physiological and Psychological Consequences of Stress*

Figure 21 outlines the effects of stress on both a psychological and physiological level, and how it affects actual performance.

In nature, animals will respond to stressful demands with a 'fight or flight' response. When they feel threatened they will either fight you and become aggressive or will move away from the situation, fleeing from the threat. Maybe there have been times during a match when you have felt like responding in a 'fight or flight' way. The eliciting of this response is normal and in line with nature's way of protecting us. However, top sportsmen are expected to deal with stress advantageously and not to respond in a manner that affects performance. In fact, it is those sportsmen who successfully deal with the pressures of competition who eventually reach the top.

During stress the body undergoes spontaneous and involuntary change. It gets ready for action in the situation. Muscle tone changes. Muscles tighten, with increased tension. With it the

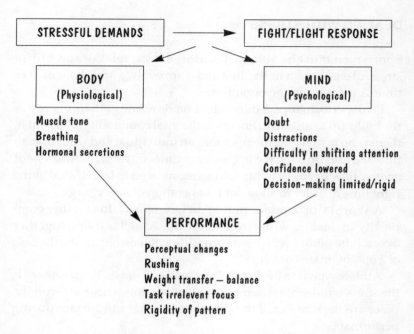

*Figure 21: Body-mind changes during heightened stress and the effects on actual performance*

breathing pattern and rhythm is affected. Breathing becomes more rapid and shallow. There are also hormonal secretions that occur. The adrenalin pumps. These are all natural changes as one gets ready for the demands that need to be confronted on the field. Stress occurs in the build-up to an important match and occurs during competition where there is intense pressure. The important thing to remember is that physical body changes will occur spontaneously. It therefore becomes important to work at increasing your body awareness.

On a psychological level, internal doubt starts creeping in. You doubt whether you are able to execute the normal sort of activity that you have done in the practice sessions. You doubt whether you have the ability to be successful in the actual match situation. Internal distractions enter the mind. This affects concentration. You may feel out of control and have little inner confidence in your own abilities. Athletes need a clear, calm and quiet mind to make decisions on the field. Under stress, decision making becomes rigid and predictable. The mind 'shrinks' and there is limited perception. Creative and spontaneous flow become restricted.

## The Effects of Stress on Performance

The consequences of these physiological (body) and psychological (mind) changes feeds into actual performance. There are a number of **signals** during performance that reflect that the athlete is under stress. Become aware of these signs. These will put you in touch with your own stress level during performance.

- A player under stress undergoes **perceptual changes**. For a golfer, a three metre putt may 'seem' like a five metre putt. Perceptually the distance seems very different. A rugby player who is relaxed and in the flow, may see a gap and take it, whereas a player under stress will not venture in trying to go through the gap. These emotional changes will affect the information that your senses are taking in. In addition, the processing of sensory information is slowed. It takes longer to assimilate all the necessary incoming visual and auditory information.
- **Rushing** occurs. Athletes will unconsciously speed up and rush through the situation. There is no smooth flow. Timing goes. One tries to hit the ball harder than normal and quicker than normal. Everything seems to be speeding up. The opposition appear to be coming onto you quicker. The ball seems to be going quicker. You are also rushed for time.
  The feeling of rushing can be equated with the jerky movements of people that one sees in the old silent movies. Everything is speeded up. There is no time to rest, no time to breathe. In order to slow the interactive process, an athlete needs to become aware of the flow of activity. Rushing is a clear message that you are in the wrong place at the wrong time.
- **Weight** and **balance** are affected under stress. Both mind and body lose their balance. Your body becomes unbalanced while trying to perform. Balance in the body is the most fundamental element for successful execution of any athletic tasks. In addi-

tion, one's body centre (situated approximately 10cm behind the navel), becomes unsteady. You lose your foundation.

In hockey, for example, it is important that you are balanced when making a tackle. If not, you may find yourself being pushed back on your heels when defending. This reduces physical manoeuvrability and you will easily be beaten. If you become aggressive, you push your physical centre forward. This may lead to you committing yourself to a tackle at the wrong time. Physical centredness and balance is vital for the execution of complex action in space. Both your physical and psychological centres can shift when under pressure. Before making a speech, for example, there is often the feeling that your heart is pumping in your throat. In a sense, your centre has risen and in the process has made you top-heavy and unstable. Feeling unstable can result in careless mistakes. In addition, being unbalanced reduces awareness, which may prevent you from assimilating the incoming cues and messages from the environment. A way to remedy this would be to practise Tai Chi. Being physically balanced in movement is the fundamental focus of Tai Chi. The slow movement in action allows one to become highly tuned and sensitised to your physical centre. Slight changes in balance are immediately felt, and the execution of simple action becomes extremely difficult.

- **Task irrelevant focus** occurs. The athlete starts focusing on situations that are irrelevant to the tasks that he has to execute. Task irrelevant focus can be externally or internally directed. An example of external irrelevance, would be the energy and concern expended on umpires, crowd, climatic conditions; those people and/or conditions over which the athlete has no control, or is unable to influence. Elements in the crowd, for example, may affect concentration, distracting the athletes from the task of performance.

Internal irrelevance is all the thoughts that are linked with your own performance, but that interfere with your achieving your goal. An example of such a thought would be 'I wonder if I am capable or good enough'. This doubt uses up a great deal of internal energy. It is actually task-irrelevant, since the athlete should have his focus on the actual task, and on the process of being able to achieve success in simple action.

- **Poor decision-making** by an athlete is due to an overload of stress. Decisions become predictable. The same mistakes are repeated over and over again. The athlete does not seem to be able to learn from his mistakes. It is necessary for elite athletes to be flexible in thinking. Being able to quickly sum up a situation and adjust to the demands in a creative way is the hallmark of a good sportsman.

Stress limits the mind. In a sense, stress squeezes and reduces the thinking options. Mentally, athletes freeze under stress. The body becomes immobilised. Stress becomes like a suffocating blanket. It strangles the athlete.

As stress continues to influence the athlete, there comes a point where it breaks down the focus of the athlete. The consequence of this is the start of the vicious, self-feeding, downward spiral of performance.

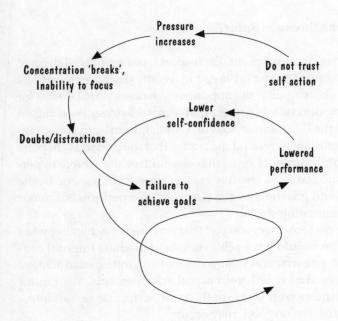

*Figure 22: Downward spiral of performance*

As stress increases, it breaks down concentration, doubts increase, distractions occur, you do not achieve the goals that you have set for yourself, not achieving your goals means that performance is lowered. As you become aware that you are not performing to your expectations, you start losing confidence in your abilities, and in the process you now start feeding into this spiral and further increase the stress load. You now feed into your own stress. You provide further fuel to escalate the downward spiral.

From a psychological viewpoint, the main objective is to exert pressure on the opponent. In interactive team games, the objective is to try and fragment the opposition's team wholeness. Once this has occurred, the fragmented part can be isolated with no support. Then, the downward spiral is likely to be deepened since the player will be unable to refocus his energy on a simple achievable goal. The player will then have to cope with an increase in his own stress level, as well as having to deal with the opposition's pressure.

### What Causes Stress in Sport?

Sport is played for enjoyment. Each sport has a set of well defined interactional rules. Sport is played in a context where the athlete can test his skills against the opponent. An obsessional desire for achievement for results is a factor that increases stress. Focusing on the score in the desperation to win, will heighten your inner tension. It is important to remind the reader that the previous chapters outlined a philosophy of sport that should free the athlete to perform with spontaneous creative energy flow. In other words, the way your mind has defined the nature of competition is a major factor in accentuating stress.

If during performance, you feel that you are not achieving what you think you should have achieved, an immediate internal conflict arises. Your own expectations of what you intended to achieve are not in accordance with your actual achievements. Your mind may start blaming your body for the poor performance – an internal dialogue of 'I'm no good' may occur.

In his first Currie Cup cricket match, Jonty Rhodes scored a century for Natal. 'In my first season, there were no expectations on me. You do not realise how difficult it really is. But, doing well puts pressure on you. In my second season, I went through a stage of wanting to do really, really well, but I wasn't succeeding. But you could not recognise what situation you were in because there was so much pressure on.'

Bruce Fordyce contends that an athlete should not be too intense about his performance. Bruce believes that a large part of his success in running the Comrades is his ability to relax and 'switch off' in the first half of the race, yet still be aware of the other front runners. 'I don't ever think that I am going to win. You have to prepare yourself for a long hard struggle. Not to say "I am going to win", but that "I am going to do well – I am going to be up there at the end." To say you are going to win is putting too much pressure on yourself.'

Important matches heighten stress. Your mind makes distinctions between a club match, a provincial match, and an international match. The actual sport never changes. This is why sportsmen perform remarkably well in practice sessions and are unable to transfer this standard into an actual match. The competition situation seems to be important. There is always the feeling of being judged by the standards of your play. One's own self concept and inner feelings towards oneself, become linked with the results that one obtains in the match.

For elite sportsmen, winning is linked to financial rewards and sponsorships. Professional athletes depend on these remunerations to live. This adds pressure. Sport is work. Performance is judged by results. The only successful result becomes the end result of winning. The public do not support losers. The media and advertising world further increase the focus on the sportsman. Television brings his performance into everyone's home. The spotlight is on. There is no place to hide.

## Dealing with Stress in Competition

The following suggestions can help alleviate the build up of debilitating stress. You need to incorporate some of these methods during your own performance. Try and experiment with these suggestions, and if necessary, modify the concepts in order to suit your own unique needs.

- Do not link sporting results with your self image. Your own self worth should be independent of how you are performing. Sport has been designed to test and challenge you. This is the nature of sport.
- Do not focus on results when things are going badly. Instead, focus on your involvement during play. Become interested in the flow. Connect to this flow. Set yourself a very simple goal in mind (not 'I must win'). Set out to achieve this simple goal in the territory. For example, 'I want to keep my head still when I hit the ball', or 'I want to give a simple, obvious pass and then run off the ball'. If achieved, these simple goals provide you with the best chance of achieving success. A solid foundation is being set. In other words, remember to remain simple in the journey.
- In highly interactive sports such as rugby, football and hockey, the mind needs to prepare itself when you do not have the ball. Become aware and connected with your fellow players. Scan the space that you are in. This should be done before receiving the ball. Once the ball has been received, you need to spontaneously execute the action that you believe is right. At that moment, the mind does not think, the body just responds.
- In highly interactive sport, stress breaks down the interpersonal links and support systems. In particular, communication between players breaks down on the field when a team is under stress. There is a heavy quietness. It is vital that players keep on talking to each other, during intense pressure. The communication should be supportive and of an organisational type. By this I mean talking that retains the structure, shape or organisation of the team is very important. Emotional support also helps reduce stress levels. Be careful of giving critical comments. These will most likely escalate the tensions.
- Where there is time to think in sport (as with golf), stress is likely to be triggered and then heightened by an evaluation of action. 'Do instructions' from mind to body increase physiological tightening. Notice the emergence of self-talk in stressful situations. Try to remain quiet and calm in mind, by creating an

image of calmness/stillness. I often suggest working on an image of a calm clear lake, that reflects the surrounding vegetation; as well as allows one to look into the still water. There is no wind and no ripples. The mind is able to re-focus and calm itself, if it has an image to focus on and look at.

- Become aware of your body during performance. This may seem strange to you, but the majority of sportsmen under stress are not even aware that they are under stress. When the mind connects to the body sensations, the body thanks you for taking notice. It receives a message of 'I care' from the mind. As you are reading now, stop and become aware of your body – which parts feel relaxed and which parts tense? As you get in touch with your body, do not try and consciously change the sensations. Instead, just ask your mind to remain at this awareness level. Unknowingly, this becomes a powerful way of dealing with stress.

- Focus on your breathing. This is a powerful stress reliever. In Tai Chi, relaxed focused breathing creates an inner balance. Breathing is the rhythm of life. Ask yourself to get in touch with your rhythm of breathing. What is the rhythm like? Do you want to slow the speed? How deep are you breathing? Each time you exhale, quietly say to yourself: 'relax' or 'calm'. Shallow, rapid breathing is not conducive to creating a relaxed state. During competition, there will be periods in the match where you can focus on your breathing. Even in highly interactive sports, there are always short periods during the match where you can connect to your breathing.

- Periods of deep relaxation in the days leading up to competition should be a vital part of a sportsman's mental preparation. Relaxation is a natural stress releaser. I will be covering the aspects of relaxation and music in more detail in a later section.

### Stress and the Coach

I believe that the most stressful period for an athlete is in the build up to the match. It is in this period that the athlete is in the 'waiting phase'. All the necessary preparation has been done. The athlete is prepared as best as possible. He is ready. This 'waiting phase' incorporates those last few days before the big match, as well as the final hours building up to the start of the match. Once on the field, the physical activity will naturally help relieve the inner tension. However, this may take some valuable time during the match while the athlete is still feeling tight, and in the process, may not perform to his potential.

I was acutely aware of this 'waiting phase' when I made contact with the Natal rugby team, three days before the 1990 Currie Cup final. It was important that the players did not generate inner stress and play the final over and over again in their minds before the actual kick-off. This would have resulted in unnecessary wastage of energy. In addition, the players may unknowingly be working each other up. Therefore, it becomes vitally important not to be too intense and thorough and structured during this period. I believe that, besides periods of relaxation, players should also be given enough of their own free time away from the team.

The coach always plays his match before the actual match, while the athlete plays his match on the actual day of competition. There is a mismatch of arousal and energy levels in the build-up of inner tension.

In his preparation of the players for the match, the coach must be aware of whether he is not unconsciously transferring his own tensions and concerns onto the players. The coach needs to monitor his own stress level as the build-up to competition approaches. It is recommended that coaches should spend time alone, relaxing and separating from the players. The coach needs time and the space to get clarity in his own thinking.

During the week's intensity of interprovincial hockey, I know of one coach who has his own physical training programme of long distance running as a method of remaining inwardly balanced. It is during this period, that he is able to release built-up tension on a mental level through physical activity. He also reviews his own thinking about team strategies for important matches during his run. Further, the team has its own space to develop their own competence and problem-solving, separate from him.

Coaches need distance from the hurly-burly of taking all the responsibility. Coaches need to rest. They need to formulate their

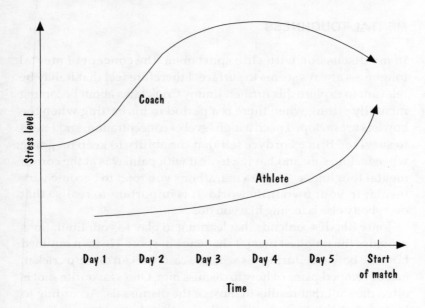

*Figure 23: 'Mismatch' in stress levels of the coach and athlete leading up to competition*

own stress-release programme (in what ever form). Players unconsciously sense inner tensions in a coach. This may disrupt the energy flow of the athlete.

Ian McIntosh, the Natal rugby coach, contends that the relaxation sessions I had conducted for the team in the build-up to the 1990 Currie Cup final, were the most beneficial aspect of my involvement with the side. 'I have never felt so relaxed before a match, as I felt on that day. I am convinced it rubbed off onto the players,' Ian said.

When the actual day of competition arrives do not escalate new input for the players to deal with. Coaching now stops. A coach can unintentionally interfere with the natural energy flow of the athlete. On the day of competition, the coach unconditionally lets go. He trusts in the ability of the players. As a coach, he has done all the hard work in getting the athlete to this point. Now he releases control. There is no panic. Instead, the coach maintains his own inner calmness and balance.

## MENTAL TOUGHNESS

In my discussion with elite sportsmen, the concept of mental toughness always seems to surface. I therefore feel that it may be relevant to explore this further. Jimmy Cook talks about becoming mentally strong when there is a period in his batting when the bowlers are on top. 'I need a high level of concentration, and I need to survive.' Bruce Fordyce felt that the ability to keep on going when feeling sore and having to deal with pain, was at the core of mental toughness. 'In ultra marathons you tend to become very insular in your own little world. It is important to realise that everybody else is feeling like you do.'

Jonty Rhodes contends that learning to play to your limitations provides the toughest mental challenge in sport. He then outlined how the bowlers, during his second season of Currie Cup cricket, had developed plans of how to dismiss him. One's favourite shot is often the shot that results in most of the dismissals. According to Jonty, being able to focus on not playing that shot under pressure is the core of mental toughness.

Each sport demands something unique from the athlete in those highly stressful and taxing moments. For a batsman, it seems to be the ability to increase concentration and maybe be tight regarding the shots played, taking no risk. For a bowler, mental toughness will be most needed when the batsman is on top. Bowling on extremely hot days, on a wicket that is not helping the bowler will require mental strength. The ability to keep on bowling the correct length and direction, in order to maintain the pressure on the batsman, demands extra resources from the bowler.

Squash is a physically demanding sport. It is highly explosive. In discussing mental toughness with Jonathon Leeb, a top South African squash player, the three P's emerged. Pain, patience and pressure. There is a dynamic connection between the P's which feed into performance. For example, the more patient you are during a rally, the more pressure you are likely to put on your opponent, but the more pain you have to endure yourself. The tolerance of pain while trying to maintain the pressure on the opponent, requires an inner mental strength. But the ability to maintain the pressure on the opponent, is dependent on being patient during a rally, which is linked to one's pain threshold and tolerance level. During a tough long rally, the mind is almost at breaking point: pressure on the opponent heightens the inner physical pain, yet during the rally, an inner patience is also necessary to decide on the type of shots to play. One has to minimise the potential for error.

Brian Mitchell generates his mental toughness from the knowledge that he has physically worked hard in training sessions in the build-up to a World title fight. Brian expands further 'that extra bit of work is what will pull you through. I had that bit of extra reserve. When I went down, I got up. I knew that my opponent was going to get tired and I knew that I was going to get him.' Physical toughness creates mental toughness due to the interdependent connection between mind and body. When mind and body become one and integrate, the mind picks up vital cues from the body (and vice-versa). Brian just knew that he could and would be able to get up, if he was knocked down.

A provincial long jumper stated that if another competitor had jumped a distance that was further than she had achieved, then a mental toughness was needed to outjump the opponent in the next jump. 'You need to prove to yourself and to the other competitors that you are up to it,' she said. In discussion with her, I wanted to know whether this may result in her trying too hard to achieve and in the process cause both body and mind to tighten and tense. She agreed that this conscious desire to outjump the opposition may inadvertently hinder her performance.

This introduced a more complex angle to mental toughness. Mental toughness needs an element of relaxedness in it, so that one is able to remain inwardly balanced during the performance. Be careful of trying to prove something to your opponent. This may result in mistakes or unforced errors. In other words, mental toughness requires a calmness, together with an increased determination.

In order to develop your own mental toughness, take time to reflect on how you respond to pressure situations when things are not going well. Remaining focused on your goal is a sign of mental strength. It does not matter how this is achieved (using whatever thought process). The important issue is how this is transferred into sporting action.

Team sports such as hockey, soccer and rugby present more complex difficulties regarding individual mental toughness. During periods of pressure in highly interactive sport, the player becomes dependent on help and support from fellow players. In rugby the hooker, for example, is dependent on the ability of the props to be physically solid in the scrum, so that the ball can be hooked. Invariably, when there is a period of intense stress and downward flow of performance, the interdependent connections between the players are broken. What then occurs is that players start complaining (verbally or just in thought) about the performance of other team mates. The focus shifts from self (my simple goal) to concern about somebody else. When this happens, performance in the team declines remarkably. When the going gets tough in teams, you should have only one concern. Concern yourself with achieving that simple goal. Everyone needs to turn inwardly in the team. Everyone needs to take care of himself. This is my understanding of mental toughness in highly dynamic team sports.

This was the basis of the mental preparation of the Natal rugby team for the 1990 Currie Cup final. 'When the going gets tough, think of your own specific simple goal'. Each player had a clear goal in his mind before walking onto the field. The toughness was being able to apply his mind to that goal during intense pressure, and not to become distracted with all the other activity around him. This is sometimes easier said than done.

In the 1992 Currie Cup rugby final against Transvaal, the Natal players had to be mentally tough to ensure success. The Transvaal team had had natural energisers that aroused motivation. Both their captain and coach were going to retire after the final. This generates tremendous sentimentality and meaning in a team. Further, the Transvaal coach, Harry Viljoen, had taken the team to consecutive finals in his two years as coach. This was a remarkable achievement. He had instilled an enthusiasm for rugby in the Transvaal team. In addition, history had shown that Transvaal had won the Currie Cup in 1952 and 1972. Would history be repeated in 1992? I was acutely aware of this historical pattern. I have respect for cosmic pattern.

The mental toughness of the Natal players had at its core commitment and courage. The players had become aware of the psychological obstacles they had to contend with. There were also high expectations of success from the Natal media and supporters, which added extra pressure on the team. In addition, the team had to deal with its own history of expectation when they had beaten Northern Transvaal against all odds in the 1990 final. It was important that the players did not look back. All the players had recognised that the 1992 final would be tougher mentally because 'the second time round is always tougher'. The final score of 14 – 13 to Natal reflected the toughness of the journey upon which all 30 players had embarked.

## RELAX TO PERFORM

A relaxed sportsman is spontaneous and fully aware of his actions and involvement during performance. Body movements are smooth, yet precise. Garfield (1985) states that peak performance is largely attributed to being both physically and mentally relaxed. Mental relaxedness reflects itself in an inner calmness and quietness. Time slows, decisions are not consciously made but are spontaneous, without thought. Being physically relaxed allows the body to flow. There is ease of movement.

Relaxation should not be confused with a casualness or 'who cares' attitude. Nothing could be further from the truth. Relaxation provides one with an inner calmness and quiet confidence during performance. The relaxed sportsman trusts himself in the situation.

Due to the demands of top sport, athletes do not need heightened motivation in the build-up to an important match. The definition of the importance of the match will naturally motivate and activate the energies of a player. In my experience, the opposite is required: periods of quietness, relaxed focusedness. During relaxation, old tensions are released and new creative energy is generated. It is this creative energy that will be used in performance.

Being a Christian, Jonty Rhodes has come to relax through prayer. He is able to find an inner peace in the process. 'I realise that it is not in my hands in what happens. This takes the pressure off me,' states Jonty. He continues, 'I also do not try and mentally prepare for a match. I leave it as late as possible. This reduces the pressure.' Jonty has had to go through a tough learning experience in order to get to his present state of thinking. He believes that his second season in Currie Cup cricket was physically and mentally draining because of his own intensity and desperate desire to do well. 'I can still remember playing Transvaal at the Wanderers over Christmas. Being next in, I became violently sick due to the pressure. I had to ask Trevor Madsen to go in to bat. It took me over half an hour to recover. I don't ever want to go through that again.'

### A Simple Technique

Let us now discuss a simple method of relaxation. During the relaxation, do not try and force your body to relax. No prescription should occur. Instead, your body will naturally relax if you allow it the opportunity to rest. Provide the necessary space and time to relax. Relaxation is safe and normal.

1. Find yourself a place where you will not be disturbed.
2. Now either sitting in an upright position or lying down with arms and legs uncrossed, close your eyes and ask your mind to get in touch with your body. Ask your mind to do a mental checklist of those parts of your body that feel tense and tight and those parts that feel relaxed. Start at your head, and slowly move down your body. Do not try and change any body sensations. Instead, become aware of body sensations. Do not force any bodily change. All you are doing is connecting mind with body. You are providing the mind-body link.
3. Now focus on your breathing. Breathing is the rhythm of life. Get in touch with your own rhythm. Remember that shallow rapid breathing increases tension and tightness. Each time you exhale, quietly say to yourself: 'calm'. Each time you exhale, you allow yourself to let go . It is safe to let go. You let go of doubt and tension. You let go of control. It is safe. While breathing, work on a deep relaxed even rhythm.

'Breath is life. It symbolises the Spirit which is in you and around you. People have the idea that the life within us is unique to ourselves; that my life is different from your life. This is not correct. Life is Spirit. The same spiritual life force permeates and animates all the life forms in the world. What differs is the external containers which hold this spiritual essence.' (Galante 1981: 43)

4. Now ask your mind to drift off to a safe place, where there are no pressures or responsibilities. There are no demands in this quiet safe place. Take careful note of your place of safety in your mind's eye. If you do not have a quiet safe place, ask your mind to create such a place. It can be near a river or in the mountains. You should feel safe, comfortable and confident in this place.
5. A further way to enhance relaxation is to listen to instrumental music with a slow calming rhythm. The beat of the music should not arouse you. Ask your mind to drift off in the music. Move gently with the flow. Lose yourself in the music. (I will cover this topic in greater detail in a later section.)

There is no specific duration for the relaxation. Thirty minutes of quietness will allow for regeneration of creative energy. Old tensions will have been released. The reader is referred to Herbert Benson's book *The Relaxation Response* (1975) for further exploration of the state of relaxation. I have always taken the view that there is no specific one right way to relax. Individuals vary according to their own bodily responses in the relaxation process. Use whatever method works for you.

The timing of relaxation in the build-up to competition needs careful consideration. There are two aspects to note: firstly there is the deep relaxation that is necessary in the days leading up to the important match. This relaxation will allow you to release built-up inner tensions and stresses. Secondly, short periods of quietness may be necessary just before the match or during actual competition. These two aspects are now examined in more detail.

## Leading up to the Important Match

A 30/45 minute period of relaxation is necessary in the days leading up to an important match. You should relax on at least three occasions in the week leading up to the competition. During this relaxation, you will be releasing built-up tension that may be occurring due to your worries concerning your performance in the big match. On the other hand, only one period of relaxation the night before the competition may actually make you feel lethargic on the day, if you have not had any other relaxation period. Therefore avoid doing deep relaxation the night before the match. It is important to build a relaxation programme into the weeks leading up to the competition.

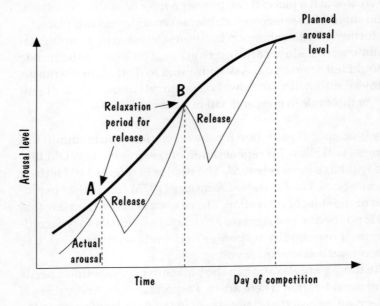

*Figure 24: Periods of relaxation to release the rapid increase in arousal build-up to competition*

The dark graph reflects the planned arousal increase of the athlete that will give him the best energetic and physiological state for peak performance. The light graph represents the actual arousal and tension of the athlete as he approaches the day of the competition. Notice that at points A and B, the actual arousal will shoot through the planned build up. If this does happen, the athlete will be wasting psychic energy and in the process will start building up inner tension that will affect the performance on the day of competition. The athlete needs to maintain a dynamic balance between relaxation and the inner arousal that builds up as the day of competition draws closer. At points A and B, the athlete will benefit from doing deep relaxation. The relaxation will release old tensions and in the process lower the arousal build-up. This dynamic process of build-up and release needs to be carefully thought through by both coach and athlete. The athlete needs to understand his own energy flow and activity, so that meaningful release of tension can occur. Timing is vital.

During your relaxation, you can do a visualisation of your performance. Visualisation means seeing, hearing, smelling and feeling yourself in your mind's eye. Visualisation is most beneficial during a relaxation. Your mind helps your body become aware of the requirements during the performance.

There are two types of visualisation. Firstly, from an external position see yourself performing on a television screen. Watch yourself in movement. You are the observer of your own performance. Create in your mind the situation in the match that you wish to deal with. Focus your attention on how you are performing. Create a perfect performance in your mind's eye. Further, notice how your opponents are playing. Take in information about the field setting and the crowd. In a sense, you are pre-empting a match play situation in your mind's eye. You are preparing your body.

A second way to visualise is to actually feel yourself perform. This is a kinesthetic, internal visualisation, where you feel the movements.

### On the Actual Day of the Match

On the actual day of the competition, one could do relaxation. This depends on you. The nature of this relaxation is totally different from the deep relaxation as explained previously. Therefore I like to suggest a time-out period for athletes, about two to three hours before the start of competition. In this period, you need to spend some quiet time refocusing on your goals. You are gathering your thoughts in a quiet way.

Focus on a very simple goal that you wish to achieve at the start of the match. Keep it simple. While you are sitting quietly away from the hustle and bustle of others, focus on your breathing: it should have a deep rhythm. In this relaxation before a match, you do not want to go too deeply into a relaxed state, because it takes time to recover from the relaxation. Instead, you have removed yourself from the excitement and energy of the presence of others. This activity of others may be working against your own rhythm and energy flow. By taking this period of quietness, you are conserving your own energy: it is not dissipated by the talk and expectations of others as the tension at the start of the competition builds.

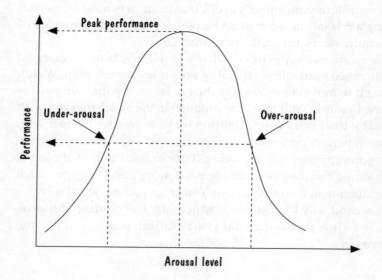

*Figure 25: Proper arousal level to ensure peak readiness for performance*

Figure 25 shows the bell shape of arousal and psychological readiness. On the actual day of competition, the athlete will need to time his arousal so that he gives himself the best possible chance for peak performance. Feeling lethargic before the match, for example, may in actual fact reveal that you have gone over the top. Too much psychic energy may have been used before the match. This energy can never be recaptured. Therefore, re-correction may not be possible, and will result in lowered performance. You will need to monitor your own energy flow. Get to know your own internal pattern and rhythm. A dynamic balance always exists between relaxation and arousal. I refer to this balance as psychological readiness. You are aroused, yet relaxed. You are determined and focused, yet your movements are free and creative.

During actual performance, there may be time for you to detach from the activity. When this is possible, focus on your breathing in order to help your body to relax. In addition, your mind could focus on a simple goal. Re-read the section on dealing with stress during competition, in order to introduce aspects of relaxation into your actual play.

## MUSIC – A RELAXER AND AROUSER : TRANSCENDING OBSTACLES

This section on music should be examined and linked to my comments regarding relaxation leading up to competition.

There are a number of fundamental reasons why I use music in the mental preparation of athletes or teams:

- Listening to music is a right-brain experience which links with sports movement and flow. The table below distinguishes between left and right brain functioning (Zdenek, 1985).

| Left-Brain Specialisation | | Right-Brain Specialisation | |
|---|---|---|---|
| **Verbal:** | Language, reading writing | **Nonverbal:** | Images |
| | | **Spatial:** | Perception of location |
| **Analytical:** | Logical, rational | | |
| **Literal:** | Understands literal interpretation | | Spatial relationships |
| **Linear:** | Processes sequentially One step at a time | **Holistic:** | Evaluates whole problem at once |

| Left-Brain Specialisation | Right-Brain Specialisation | |
| --- | --- | --- |
| Mathematical | **Metaphoric:** | Imagery |
| | **Musical** | |
| | **Imaginative:** | Fantasy, stories |
| | **Artistic** | |
| | **Emotional:** | In touch with feelings |
| | **Spiritual:** | Worship, mysticism |
| | **Dreams:** | Metaphoric internal poet |

- An 'obstacle' is created by mind in such a way as not to allow mind to solve it (refer to the section on Problem and Solution in Chapter 4). In other words, an obstacle may not respond to rational, analytical thinking. Obstacles are stubborn. Resolution will therefore require a different approach. Music creates a relaxed atmosphere in which to focus on the problem, and provides the vehicle with which to by-pass the problem.
- The music allows each individual to work on his own visualisation in a meaningful way in a team context. During a piece of music, each player can be asked to focus on a particular team and/or individual issue that needs further exploration during visualisation (see Gawain, 1982).
- Music allows for relaxation to occur. Periods of relaxation for release of stress and tension is vital. Visualisation, focus and flow of movement and a quietening of the mind, allows for the regeneration of creative energy.
- Behaviour is dependent on the physical and mental state that one is in. Internal representations (mental picture) and physiology (body sensation) are the factors that create our state (Robbins, 1986). Internal representations and physiology work together in a cybernetic or circular loop. They feed into each other. Music is able to get an athlete into the correct relaxed physiological state, in order to perform certain sporting actions.

## The Meaning in Music

Music can be used to help motivate or relax. Music can also provide new insights to difficulties that an athlete may be experiencing.

Let us assume that you tend to be too uptight during performance. Suppose you wish to relax more while you are competing. Choose a piece of music that best represents relaxation for you.

While listening to this music in the weeks leading up to competition, you can visualise (seeing and feeling) yourself being relaxed on the field. This music can also be used just before the start of the match, in order to help you feel relaxed and confident. During your actual performance, you could quietly hum the song to yourself.

As an exercise, choose different pieces of music to represent:

- confidence
- aggression
- calmness
- relaxedness
- toughness
- determination
- happiness
- depression

The experiential feelings that are evoked while listening to music are subjective. 'Calming' music for you, may feel like 'depressing' music to somebody else.

I was consulted by a professional golfer who felt that he had lost the rhythm in his swing. After some discussion, I recommended that he go home and find a piece of music that best reflects the rhythm of his old swing (which he had wanted to recapture). Further, he had to find a piece of music that reflected his speed and flow of his present swing as he was experiencing it at the moment.

In the next consultation, we played the two pieces of music in order to gain more insight into the rhythm of his swing. As we listened to the music, we compared the beat and rhythm. The music was best able to indicate the nature of his old, smooth swing compared to his present fast and rushed swing. I suggested that he listen to the music that reflected the smooth, easy swing every day for a week. While listening to this music, I asked him to visualise himself swinging to the beat of the music. This allowed him the opportunity to reconnect to that easy comfortable swing.

Bruce Fordyce uses music in his mental preparation for the Comrades. He states that he always has a theme song for each year of running the Comrades. While listening to this music, he spontaneously does a mental rehearsal of certain parts of the race. The music creates the sort of atmosphere that allows him to pre-plan his tactics in a relaxed way. While listening to the music, Bruce develops a positive mind-set about his race. The music makes him feel confident.

### Music to Transcend Obstacles

I now wish to examine a reflective inner process that uses music to deal with obstacles. The process allows the athlete an opportunity to detach from his difficulty, as well as to generate a creative problem-solving strategy that incorporates the intuitive right-side brain.

In order to be able to transcend the difficulty that you wish to resolve, it is important that you do not become desperate in your quest for answers. Therefore, the following are necessary attitudinal and/or behavioural elements that allow for transcendence of any obstacle:

- Relaxation
- Quieten the mind
- Visualisation and imagery
- Focus and flow
- Allow time for doubts
- Trust, no judgement, let go
- No prescription or force

These elements are at the core of creativity. Further, you will notice that some of these elements are at the heart of the psychology of being that I believe takes the athlete beyond winning. In order to explore these elements in more detail, you are referred to the chapter on 'The Psychology of Winning'.

Step 1 is a relaxation. Step 2 through to step 5 incorporates the use of instrumental music. I use different pieces of music for each of these steps. The main idea is to focus on an image in the beginning of the music, and then to allow your mind to flow with the music. Move and flow with the rhythm. Lose yourself in the music.

**Step 1:** Follow the relaxation technique as outlined previously.

**Step 2:** Obtain an image or symbol or picture of the obstacle that you wish to work on. This has been the obstacle that has been holding you hostage. Just focus on the obstacle. Do not try and solve it. Allow the image into mind without the necessity to respond to it.

**Step 3:** Recall any happy or confident time. Re-experience those feelings. Take careful note of how you were behaving, communicating, moving. Relive these feelings now. The experience that you recall should enter mind without force. It can be any time in the past, where there was an ease in the way that you responded and behaved in the situation.

**Step 4:** Now go back to your obstacle and in your mind's eye move around the image. See and feel yourself moving. Keep moving. Dance if you wish. Do not touch or interfere with the obstacle. Just move around. Jump over or crawl under the obstacle. Explore the obstacle while moving. Move with the rhythm of the music.

**Step 5:** Now allow your mind the freedom to drift. Do not hold onto any specific thought or feeling. Allow any thought to enter mind. Do not entertain any thought for too long. Just drift. Allow yourself the freedom to explore any idea. These ideas will not necessarily be connected to your obstacle.

Listen to the rhythm of the music without trying to obtain images. I use four pieces of different music for steps 2, 3, 4 and 5. Each different piece of music acts as a punctuation for the steps in the process. From a personal perspective, I find the music of Andreas Vollenweider, a harpist, relaxing and flowing. You need to experiment yourself. Remember to link your own energy flow with the

flow presented in the music. If it feels good to you, you have connected to the rhythm of the music. It will then prove to be beneficial.

### The Psychological Benefits of the Model

The model as outlined above has a number of benefits for the athlete. In particular, music creates the sort of atmosphere that allows
the athlete to journey in mind without restriction. More specifically, the process :

- Bypasses analysis. Music quietens the analytical and rational
  mind.
- Breaks the 'more of the same' solution pattern that was discussed
  in Chapter 4. The loop between the defined obstacle and the
  attempted solution is broken. This allows for newness to emerge.
- Transcends the definition of the problem. Remember that the
  problem definition will only allow certain possible solutions. The
  problem frame limits one's perception. The imagery obtained in
  the listening to the music allows for new insights. Music allows
  transcendence, much in the same way as being in a trance.
- Does not prescribe and force ideas. This allows freedom to
  explore the obstacle in a creative manner.
- Externalises the obstacle. Detachment occurs which allows the
  person to be an observer of self.
- Allows visualisation and imagery. Music stimulates the right-
  brain, which in turn stimulates imagery.
- Provides a context for relaxation and release of tension.
- Ensures regeneration of creative energy.
- Provides rhythm in order for flow to occur.
- Allows the evolution of multiple realities to occur at one given
  time in a group context. This is in line with the principles of eco-
  logic that were previously discussed. Each athlete works on
  his/her own obstacle in a meaningful way.

On re-reading what I have outlined in the model, I am acutely
aware that there may seem to be big gaps in my attempted explanation of how music can be utilised to enhance your performance.

This is because I have no music to play for you. Words and music operate on different levels. This model can be used in dealing with any problem or obstacle that is hindering your flow. While listening to your music, remember to follow the steps as described. Further, do not rush and attempt to find a solution. Do not become desperate. Instead, lose yourself in the music.

## IMAGERY

Once in consultation with a team, I had the feeling that I had not connected to the core issues that the players were struggling with. In one of those moments, I spontaneously asked the team to stop the discussion. I handed out crayons and blank pieces of paper. I then asked them to draw for me an image or symbol that tells me something about the team. I put on my music, and allowed them to formulate a meaningful symbol.

On completion of the drawings there was a sense of relief in the group. It seemed that they had suddenly tapped meaningful information that could not be elicited verbally. Each symbol had an individual meaning. Each image was unique, yet told one something about the whole. Individual and team were connected in the symbol.

Since each individual symbol is a private unique expression, I asked whether they would object if they stuck their images on the wall. I then asked them to pretend that they were in an art gallery. Each player had to move around and look at the pictures. Each picture was unconsciously telling each individual something about self and something about team. In a way, one felt as if the context was tapping the unconscious of the team. Each image reflected the relationship that existed between players.

It is meaningless to try and describe what energy and meaningful dialogue this process unleashed. This could only have been felt in that unique interpersonal context. What is important, is that each individual in the team felt freer individually, and more connected interpersonally. The performance in the important match that was being prepared for, reflected creative and committed effort. The end result was extremely satisfying for both coach and team. A synergy was achieved in the process.

Images can also be thought of as concepts/ideas as was discussed within the framework of quantum physics, in the section on energy flow. An image presents the individuals in a team with a 'particle' that radiates wave-like meaning about a situation or about the team. Each individual player creates his own meaning in the connection with the images that are presented by other members of the team. A unifying theme will start emerging in the team. It is this unifying theme that will generate the energy for a possible quantum leap in performance.

Imagery bypasses words. It allows the athlete the opportunity to explore the situation in more complexity. Since sport is a nonverbal right-brain exercise, the process in unleashing meaningful images matches the right-brain activity of sport.

I often get approached by sportsmen who state that they do not feel confident. They request help in gaining more confidence. In a relaxed state, I ask them to get an image that reflects confidence. I ask them to draw this image. I get them to take the image home and stick it on a wall where they can see the image for at least 10 minutes a day. Unconsciously, they need to connect to the image that they had drawn. To add further complexity, I may also ask them to get an image of themselves lacking confidence. Now they need to study the differences in the images without trying to rationally get any solution. Unconsciously, there will be meaning. It is the unconscious that provides images. Images always tell one more than a verbal description.

For the 1992 Currie Cup rugby final, the Natal players had discussed the necessity of having courage during the match. As a way to generate further meaning for the players, I asked them to draw an image that best reflects courage. As the players drew their images, a oneness between left-brain (verbal understanding) and right-brain (intuitive and nonverbal) was being achieved. This process created more mental connections for the players, regarding the complexity of the phenomenon of courage.

### Images as Reflections of Problem, Solution and Context

Like dreams, images may not fully reflect what the individual may believe that they represent. If an athlete obtains an image/symbol (call it image A) that represents his problem, another image (call it image B) that reflects his possible solution, and a third image (call it image C) to represent the interpersonal situation or group that he finds himself in; then the following assumptions need to be made in trying to understand the image. These assumptions will also allow creative problem-solving by the right-brain (from whence the images were created). Further, these assumptions make it more difficult for the analytical left-brain to interfere with, in its quest to get more understanding. Some of these assumptions may appear to contradict themselves. This is due to the contradictory nature of images. It is also in line with how contradictory the unconscious really is.

- The images obtained do not necessarily reflect what the analytical left-brain had intended. In other words, the problem image may in fact be pointing to a possible solution more than representing the actual problem.
- There is nothing definite about an image. For example, an image may reflect a possible future event (and not the situation or time that you may have intended). In other words, an image may be a message of an impending event.
- Images are like a movie film. Each image is like a 'freeze frame'. It tells you something about the whole story.
- Everything is connected. This is a holistic assumption. If more than one image has been created (reflecting whatever issue, or situation, or personal characteristic), then these images should not be seen as separate, independent entities. Instead they are connected in some way.
- Any image that is obtained (for whatever purpose), may contain elements of the problem, the solution, and the interpersonal context that the person finds himself in. In a sense, these parts could be reflected in the whole, in some way.
- Images change with time and place. An image of confidence today may not feel comfortable tomorrow. Instead, a different image may emerge that is more in line with the feelings of the person at that given moment in time.
- Avoid trying to analyse images. Instead, allow quiet time to sit and re-look at the image that was obtained. One needs freedom to explore the image in a creative and reflective way.

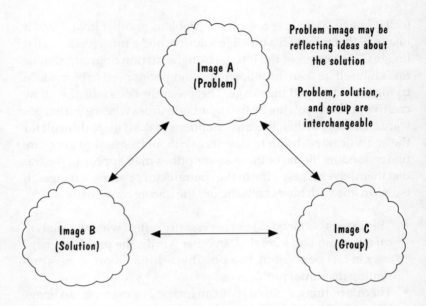

**Problem image may be reflecting ideas about the solution**

**Problem, solution, and group are interchangeable**

*Figure 26:  The interactive links (connections) that exist between images*

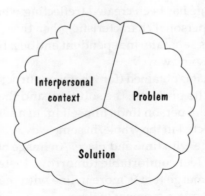

*Figure 27:  A single image contains elements of the problem, solution and interpersonal context*

Images are powerful messages that are often misinterpreted. Their power is often generated when they surface to the awareness or conscious level. Be careful of trying to analyse the image; it may prove to be frustrating. Remember that the unconscious and right-brain have created an image that may only make sense to your deep inner self. Finally, always respect the image that is obtained. It is an important reflection of yourself.

## DEVELOP YOUR OWN PROGRAMME

The main focus of this chapter has been to explore the interaction between stress/tension and relaxation. I have looked at energy flow leading up to competition, as well as how tension may disrupt this flow during actual competition. Psychic and physical energy are commodities that athletes need to nurture. Energy is extremely difficult to re-capture after it has been lost.

A dynamic balance between mind and body exists. The mind can create the necessary focus for energy to be directed towards. As an example, an image of confidence becomes the focus for directed psychic energy. On the field, physical energy gets directed towards achieving your simple goals.

Having said this, it is necessary to understand that energy is released in chunks. Performance flows in upward and downward motion. That is the nature of life. Energy is not limitless over time. Regeneration needs to occur over time.

Each individual needs to work out his own mental preparation programme. The following points are important to consider:

1. Relaxation is a vital ingredient for peak performance. Work out suitable times to relax, that fit for you. Be careful of becoming too intense in your mental preparation.
2. Your mind will need a focus on which to direct its psychic energy. During your relaxation, the mind can focus on a visualisation. See and feel yourself (in your mind's eye) performing in a certain situation. In this way, you are creating a range of playing possibilities in your mind that prepares you for action. In addition, images can also provide a meaningful focus. The focus

should not be on winning. This is the end point. Instead, ask yourself what you will need to do in order to give yourself the best chance of winning. These actions are the important building blocks.

3. Each individual's energy flow is unique. Become aware of those around you who irritate or disrupt your inner balance. If possible, keep away from people who you feel uncomfortable with. If not, learn to mentally detach from their comments. In particular, you and your coach need to work out the timing for input of coaching information. Not too much input should occur on the day of competition. This may lead to overload and unnecessary activation of mental energy. In the process, tension will increase.

4. Your inner desire to enjoy challenges during performance is a vital energy source. Top sportsmen are driven by the need to succeed. Challenges in sport will always test your psychological and physical capabilities. Focus on these challenges in your mental preparation. Challenges are energisers.

5. Develop a mental toughness appropriate to the demands of your unique sport. Mental strength implies being able to gain inspiration from within. Remaining focused on your task is a sign of mental strength.

6. Mind and body are constantly interacting. Doubts in mind should not be pushed aside. Always give time to these doubts. They are important messages from your mind. Once your mind is satisfied that you have listened to the message, it will feel more relaxed and calmer.

7. Trust yourself. Hold onto whatever works for you in improving your performance. You are unique and therefore your methods will be unique. There are no 'right' ways or 'best' techniques. The top sportsman knows what works for himself, and always uses these methods.

8. Each competition presents a moment in time for you to interact with others. Each moment is uniquely different and therefore will teach you something new about yourself. Top sportsmen never stop learning. Sport is exciting. Remain open. Remain flexible.

9. If you find yourself constantly confronting the same problem again and again that keeps interfering with your performance

then detachment from yourself and the problem is necessary. Remember that the problem may be trying to teach you something about yourself. The persistence of the difficulty may be due to your rigid belief of how to solve the problem. This may be making things worse. Stress will then increase. Refer to the section on problem and solution (in Chapter 4), and using music to transcend obstacles.

## CHAPTER 6

# Beyond Sport

**Beyond Sport** can be seen as a chapter where important issues are explored without fear of boundaries or restrictions. I have decided to focus on three topics that do not have much in common. However, the issues have confronted and challenged my own values and beliefs concerning sport and life. Therefore, the choice of focus has not been random. The issues have been especially pertinent to me as a South African.

The first issue that goes beyond sport, yet is still connected to sport, is the use of performance-enhancing drugs. As a sports psychologist working with elite athletes, I have had to confront my own views regarding healthy mental preparation and the true nature of sporting competition. The philosophy of sport as outlined in the previous chapters may seem to be idealistic and somewhat naive, and it is therefore important to confront some of the harsher realities of top sport.

The second issue of great concern, is the violence that has erupted in our country. Aggressive energy is being expressed that actually reflects deep insecurity. South Africa is in flux: a new South Africa is being moulded. In the process, there is much pain and hurt. No South African can ignore this reality: our children's future depends on our will to resolve the situation. I believe that sport can become a powerful unifying force in a changing South Africa.

The third issue on which I will focus will be to examine the concept of 'Mind in Business'. In presenting a number of business conferences, I have explored the link between healthy team functioning and healthy business functioning. As we move into the 21st century, businesses will be forced to confront their thinking concerning profit-making, employee benefits, and competition in the market place. The market cake is not getting any bigger. Resources are not unlimited. As unemployment rises, more and more stress within businesses will be experienced.

In the exploration of these issues, it is inevitable that I will take a position that is congruent with my own thinking. Therefore, concepts and ideas presented in previous chapters will no doubt surface here. There is no intention to try and provide simple answers to complex problems.

## DRUGS IN SPORT

At a recent talk to a parent group, I made the point that we were living in a 'MATRICC 'world. Briefly, MATRICC stands for:

M  –  Materialistic
A  –  Advertising
T  –  Time Pressure
R  –  Rapidly Changing
I  –  Impersonal
C  –  Competitive
C  –  Chemical Substances (Drugs)

These factors are continually impinging on our lives. They also determine the type of lifestyle that a person will lead. Modern man is being confronted with a lifestyle that undermines the inner security of self.

Modern man is lonely and disconnected in his environment. Relationships (connectedness) are fragmenting as a consequence of our MATRICC world. Time pressures, coupled with rapid change, do not allow for the building and nurturing of relationships. The impersonal nature of our existence does not encourage compassion. There is strain on that invisible link, called relationship. As compensation the striving for more and more possessions occurs. In obtaining things, however, the isolation and loneliness do not disappear. So we become more competitive, to achieve more. 'More is better' type thinking motivates the action, yet still happiness eludes us. The balance no longer exists. Crisis after crisis is nature's message to us.

Sport is embedded in society. It cannot be separated from the cultural values that are operating at a given point in time. Sport does not operate in a vacuum. Attitudes in cultural or community contexts feed into the way administrators, coaches and players respond to the challenges in the sporting arena.

The striving to improve living standards is not wrong. In fact, it is natural and inherent in man. It is part of the evolutionary process. In our society, however, success is measured by the accumulation of possessions. This is an extremely narrow definition of success. Nevertheless, material things provide one with a sense of security and achievement. Possessions can be seen (a physical thing to reflect success), as well as possessed and controlled. To some, this gives comfort.

There is tremendous personal recognition in international sport for those athletes who achieve success. Success and winning cannot be separated. In the eyes of the sporting world, 'winning well' is determined by the number of medals achieved or world records broken. Financial rewards, status, media worship and supporter followings come with the success. There are large advertising sponsorships available to elite athletes. The athlete becomes a marketable commodity. The more success achieved, the more marketable.

Having said this, I believe that elite sportsmen deserve financial rewards for the effort and time spent developing their skills. Athletes are entertainers. They give pleasure to large public followings. The excitement generated at an international rugby or football match can never be achieved without the hard work of players during practices.

The drive for achievement is linked to the self-concept of the athlete. There are some sportsmen who can only define themselves in relation to a desperate desire to prove that they can win. They will go to any means of achieving this. Psychologically, there is a distorted perception of their own self-worth. Winning is the only drug that can help them cope with their own deep insecurities and inadequate feelings of wellbeing. Winning takes on a neurotic dimension.

Pharmaceutical companies are thriving businesses in our society. Pills have been created for every conceivable problem. I believe that medication has its place; there are sophisticated treatments that improve the quality of living for those who are ill. However, due to the pressures of everyday living, drugs have offered an easy solution to difficulties that do not necessarily require medication.

Steroids and stimulants provide an athlete with excessive and unnatural energy and power that is generated through chemical and hormonal reactions in the body. These are performance-enhancing drugs. According to research, there are potentially serious physiological effects in taking these drugs. Not being a physiologist, I am not qualified and in a position to comment on the possible physiological consequences of taking these drugs. I will thus direct my focus on the psychological and interpersonal impact of taking drugs in a sporting context.

In the highly competitive sports world, the use of performance-enhancing drugs increases the possibility of winning, albeit in an unhealthy way. Therefore, an athlete taking drugs has made a clear statement of 'win at all costs'. The obsessional need to achieve success, becomes the core of his being. The implications for self, opponent, and sport are not even considered. The only focus is on an end result. In a sense, the result becomes the possession. The end result offers the security.

By taking drugs, a sportsman is making a clear statement about himself as a person. He is prepared to use whatever means to increase his chances of winning, even if it means cheating.

Athletes who use drugs are cheating. There have been a number of cases in rugby and athletics recently of athletes using some form of chemical substance. On being tested positive, the athlete attributes the traces of the drug to medication he has received for an old injury, predictably pleading 'unknowing intention'. If this is true, the medical professional who has treated the athlete, should face charges of unethical behaviour.

It all boils down to personal ethics. The fundamentals of the philosophy of sport are based on fair play. Linked to fair play, is the unquestionable trust that must exist between competitors. Competition between athletes encompasses the challenge between two opposing minds, the clash between two well-prepared bodies, and the tactical planning and strategies that each player has developed in order to overcome the obstacles that the other has consciously placed before his opponent.

One of the fundamental reasons for my love of sport is my health conscious and anti-drugs philosophy. Being part of the sporting community, I feel a deep hurt, coupled with tremendous anger when athletes go against the ethics of sporting interaction and use chemical substances to improve their chances of winning; it goes against the grain. Further, what type of role model is being created for the younger generation? What types of attitudes are being passed onto younger players who may hero worship a sportsman who uses drugs illegally?

A further consequence of drugs in sport is the pervasive suspicion that is created. Everyone is affected. Those athletes who achieve remarkable feats during performance may unjustifiably elicit 'I wonder if?' type questions from media or supporters. Unfortunately, when trust has been broken, all athletes who are clean, with healthy attitudes, may have their achievements doubted. This is not fair.

Each athlete must be held responsible for his own wellbeing. This includes all medication to be used for injury. 'Not knowing' and ignorance cannot be accepted. There is a long list of banned substances published by the international sporting body. Unfortunately, part of today's package of being a sportsman will be to become familiar with this information. When in doubt about medication, athletes should practise caution. 'Prevention is better than cure' should apply to situations where athletes intend to take medication for any particular ailment.

Drug use is threatening the fabric of sport. This cannot be allowed to happen. In this regard, sporting administrators need to review their attitudes and policies regarding the disciplining of athletes who use drugs. While punishment is not a solution to the problem of taking drugs, athletes should be aware of the severe consequences, namely suspension and the withdrawal of lucrative sponsorships.

Athletes who have used or are still using drugs are going against the true nature of sporting competition. Sport is a healthy expression of energy and activity. Rules for each sport have been developed in order for fair play to occur. No athlete should violate the deep unspoken trust and honesty that exist in sport. Honesty within, and honesty between competitors, should be at the core of sporting competitiveness.

## THE CHANGING SOUTH AFRICA

The process of establishing a new South Africa is a complex task. Integrating diverse views is not easy, yet is necessary, if synergetic wholeness is to be achieved in our country.

Our past was typified by forced separation, in order to 'protect' the diversity and differences that existed. This separation led to domination. Our society became unbalanced and in the process destructive forces of discrimination were unleashed.

Forced togetherness is equally destructive. If force has to be applied in order to control and maintain order, deep inner resentment builds up in people. Examples of such societal processes would include the old Union of Soviet Socialist Republics and, presently, the horrific war that is continuing in Yugoslavia. Forced unity in any society will result in some form of revolution, and then fragmentation into the smaller units or ethnic states that were being forced together.

A new negotiated constitution is necessary for South Africa. Care must be taken not to respond to our present crisis by reacting to past wrongs. Past global mistakes need to be our points of reference regarding our learning about how people respond to forced prescription (in whatever form).

The Convention for a Democratic South Africa (Codesa) was established in order to provide the interpersonal context to discuss whatever relevant issue emerged, regarding the formation of the new South Africa. As the process unfolds, it is well worth stating that the flow of negotiation is only maintained when the parties do not see each other as opponents who should be beaten, as in a contest. Instead, only co-operative participation can provide the context for progress. Further, if the principle of interdependent connectedness is accepted, then differences in opinion need to be integrated into a meaningful whole. The principles of ecologic offer the necessary guidance in the process of negotiation. These principles need to be protected during the bumpy journey of a negotiated settlement for a new South Africa. This will provide the only hope for a peaceful settlement.

## *The Eruption of Violence*

Change implies a shift from the old order, through a phase of chaotic disorder, to eventually finding a new order. At present, South Africa is right in the middle of such change. Large amounts of energy are being released from unexpected sources, moving in unexpected directions: some forces working together, others clashing.

The quicker the change, the greater the likelihood of chaotic violence erupting. The main intention of political violence is to unbalance the existing order. At present, there is no need for this, since the old order has started to crumble. If anything, the violence being experienced may actually hinder the movement towards a new order. People may start resisting change out of fear and insecurity.

We are experiencing horrific outbursts of violence in our communities. In the process, a culture of violence is being created, where life is not respected. Although some disruption is inevitable as a new balance is being achieved, the main political players may be unleashing destructive processes that could result in unhealthy runaways.

The violence can be viewed from a number of perspectives. Firstly, there is the expression of deep resentments that have built up over time. Secondly, there is now the expression of crude, uncontrollable and undisciplined power. Ruthless competitiveness between political parties at grassroots level is fuelling violence. Thirdly, our disadvantaged communities in the townships have been living with violence since Sharpeville 1960. Violence has become the way of trying to deal with societal issues. Force from the government at such times further rigidified the problem-solving methods of our disadvantaged people. In the process, youngsters experienced violence in everyday situations. Life and violence became one.

Although violence is an expression of power, it is also behaviour that reflects desperation and is self-fulfilling. Instead of protecting life – the only commodity that he has – the individual knows that he will lose it. (He has nothing, which in effect means that he has lost everything, and will also lose anything that he may have). Although violence is directed outward, psychologically it is fulfilling the expectation that the only commodity that the person has is at stake, and will be lost. Therefore, a context is created where loss of life is an accepted probability. A violent protagonist has no other stakes to play except his life.

The other aspect of violence is 'them/us' thinking that maintains intergroup separation. No interpersonal connection exists between the warring factions. Each group is perceived by the other as being a threat to its existence. Violent parties seek security within their own group by trying to eradicate other groups. 'We want freedom' is expressed in action that seeks to dominate other groups.

Such competitive power will always be met with an equal, yet opposite force. In this way, a balance is maintained, albeit a destructive balance. Unfortunately, an upward spiral of violence is unleashed where force is met with force in an escalating way; a runaway that gains momentum.

Stress levels are presently at breaking point in most of our communities. The only process that will have any effect on the violence, will be one that connects groups in a way where separation is respected (not forced), and where an interdependence that transcends the ethnicity is realised.

### Creating Playful Interactive Contexts

Fun and play are opposite to violence as regards their nature. Sport is a physically healthy expression of energy flow. Play provides the opportunity for people to experience themselves out of the restrictive mode of everyday living. Playful people are creative. A playful context allows for opportunities to build relationships in a non-threatening way. It allows us to stop taking ourselves so seriously.

Youngsters need to activate themselves in healthy ways. Participation in play teaches one about participation in life. Developing healthy values such as discipline, commitment and effort during activity, while receiving emotional support when tackling hardships, should be the focus of sport. Play is necessary, if one is to achieve an inner balance. Play frees one from the imposed restrictions of a situation.

Family, school, community and sporting bodies need to create convergence in thinking in order to develop the necessary sporting structures for youngsters. The United Cricket Board of South Africa is presently providing youngsters from disadvantaged communities with opportunities for play. Other sporting bodies need to take up the challenge as well. The cricket tour to the West Indies has broken more racial barriers in our communities, than any speech from a politician.

Sports administrators need to work hard at linking our communities. Sport should show politicians the way. Politicians need new insights that can be generated on the sporting fields of South Africa. On a community level, I wonder if it would be possible to organise a match between the Hostel XI and the Residents XI in Alexandra in order to try and help heal the tremendous rift between these groups. I wonder what the soccer score would be in a match between a selected Inkatha XI versus an ANC XI played at the Orlando stadium in Soweto? After the match, I wonder if it might just be possible for opposing players to connect with each other in a way that frees them from the restrictions of belonging to opposing political parties that are locked into a power game? Meaningful interactive contact between groups is necessary in order for community growth to continue.

On Sunday afternoons, there are a number of soccer matches being played in white suburbs. The clubs playing each other operate on an informal basis, and consist mainly of black players. I have watched some of these matches being played at a school near my home, and have been amazed at how sport naturally integrates interpersonal differences. This is power. Individuals are not even aware of this power. The process is natural. Playfulness provides opportunity to lose yourself: a faceless, cultureless human being in interaction, having fun. This is how children lose themselves in play.

## Pushing the Limits

Play is only possible if basic needs are satisfied. Enough food and suitable shelter are essential prerequisites for play to occur.

As time moves on, maybe there will be less and less opportunity for play and sport. Instead, energies will be directed towards survival processes. Sport could become a luxury. In fact, maybe at this very moment, sport and play is beyond the reach of some of our people who are more concerned with survival.

Play and sport provide a healthy balance to living. Yet if living becomes unbalanced, then sport has no place. That is a simple fact.

So the existence of sport and play is actually dependent on such issues as population explosion, poverty, starvation, pollution, urbanisation and violence. Sport cannot be separated from those problems existing in society. The issue of AIDS is a point in question. Certain treatment procedures have been stipulated in some sports like boxing, when a sportsman is bleeding. Referees are now wearing surgical gloves during boxing fights.

Resources are limited. There is no utopia. Sport can only continue to play a positive role in society, if each one of us confronts the challenges that are looming ahead. This becomes a shock to me as I read what I have written. The truth is that sport may become irrelevant and meaningless to us as we grapple with those issues threatening our existence.

In watching the 1992 Barcelona Olympics, I realised how unbalanced the competition had become, if you look beyond the actual day of competition and consider those deeper factors which impinge on sport. As an example, a press article in *The Star* 20th August 1992, reported that the 27 medals achieved by Australia at the Olympics, had worked out at R6 million each. In other words, Australia had invested R162 million (obtained from sponsors, Government, and the Olympic Committee) in the preparation of their Olympic athletes. I wonder what the U.S.A. had invested in their athletes?

If there are financial resources, then projects can be supported. Intensive training programmes can be scientifically developed. Elite athletes in these countries turn out to be multi-millionaires. In the eyes of these societies, they become stars with high status. These athletes do not have to work. All their time and effort is dedicated to sport. In the process, standards in performance improve. When considering all the time and effort, this is to be expected.

Being African, my mind turns to African sport. I wonder how many athletes from Somalia were at the Games? I also consider whether the Kenyan middle- and long-distance runners could have run faster (breaking more World records), if they had had a more nutritious diet from infancy.

Third world countries were competing at a disadvantage at the Olympic games. Sport cannot be separated from cultural issues and hardships. In South Africa, First and Third worlds exist right next to each other. South African sport will feel the pressure as these worlds merge and interact. The limited financial resources of sporting bodies need to be allocated in such a way as to benefit all athletes who show potential. These decisions will not be easy, as more and more needs surface. The needs have outstripped the resources.

## Common Purpose

The energy that is created on the sporting fields can provide all South Africans with a common purpose. During the World Cup cricket, a camaraderie between all South Africans was taking place in South Africa. A national pride develops during international competition.

Unfortunately, the international rugby and soccer tests that were played in August 1992 polarised our society into black/white due to issues regarding the playing of anthems at internationals. These sports have naturally fragmented into white (for rugby) and black (for soccer) supporter followings. Two anthems surfaced at these events. This was to be expected, since supporters had not been given an alternate focus of national pride and identity.

At present, there exists an uneasy vacuum regarding national symbols. The past symbols trigger different feelings for different people. This is understandable and should be respected. At this point in time, there is an urgent need for new national symbols (flag, anthem, sporting emblem). This will provide a crystallised focus for support, particularly at sports events. In the process, one national pride can start to develop.

A common purpose in a country of diversity, is not easily found. On a sports field, the common purpose of the players is to achieve their own respective goals, so that the team is given the best chance of winning. The players meet from different backgrounds, with different professional or work careers, yet are able to jell for the common purpose. The soccer or rugby fields are the playgrounds. The specific rules for interaction on the field are governed by the rules of the game. A culture of excellence can be established, if the players are dedicated and committed in whatever they do. Team synergy is generated when the group offers the individual support as well as positive feedback about himself during performance. Striving for quality in action, becomes a norm for the elite sportsman.

In society, it is important that there is a common purpose in building a future, for future generations. This is the nature of evolution. Each generation has only been given visiting rights to our planet. The test is what one does with that time.

The drive in life is towards a better quality of life. This evolutionary process is nature's way of ensuring that life continues. More complex problem-solving emerges as we are forced to adapt to more complex conditions.

Many disadvantaged people in South Africa have high expectations of improved living conditions after the new South Africa has been created. These expectations, however, may never be met. This will lead to disappointment and disillusionment.

The struggle in life is to deal with the conditions that are prevailing in a situation, in such a way as to create a process where each individual can have the freedom to be. However, the structure (mental and physical attributes) of a human system specifies how it will behave. Evolution will therefore only allow certain changes to occur in accordance with the present psychological, mental, physical attributes of the individual.

Conditions in life will always present obstacles. A commitment to becoming what you believe you are capable of, is at the core of living. As an individual's unique evolutionary process unfolds, it is important that there is something to hold onto (present circumstances), as well as having something to aim for (future focus or vision).

Each community (defined as any group of people interacting and influencing each other in any situation), needs to focus on those issues that have relevance for them. It is necessary to create plans of action with all people who are connected and/or affected by the issues.

Thinking globally and acting locally, can provide a common focus for communities. There is a diversity of expertise in communities. Processes need to be generated so that knowledge and experiences can be shared in meaningful ways. Connections need to be made in communities. Links between people need to be established.

A common purpose emerges when each person is able to bring his experiences into a situation and offer some wisdom from his own unique perspective. The commitment is to ensure a future that allows the diversity of thinking to continue.

## The Dynamic Balance in Integration

South Africa will be confronting a number of complex 'matches' that are likely to emerge over time. To briefly mention a few; 'haves' versus the 'have nots'; First World versus Third World; capitalism versus socialism. A whole range of other different 'sports' could emerge in the new South Africa. If the concept of dynamic balance is observed, then a healthy process can unfold between opposing forces. If over-extension occurs in one direction, a runaway may result which could destroy the fabric of our society.

Mind in Sport is metaphoric for Mind in Life. Sport can offer insights into healthy interpersonal functioning. What are the important interactive elements that constitute a healthy functioning whole? How are powerful synergetic groups created?

A healthy society, community or team is in dynamic balance. The new South Africa is seeking a new balance. A healthy balance can be achieved through respect and a realisation that we are all connected. This connection between the opposing forces should be in dynamic balance if a synergetic community is to be formed. Opposing forces must be integrated. All positions need to be accommodated. Each player in a synergetic team needs to feel firstly that his difference is accepted, and secondly that his difference is the 'difference that makes the difference'. This principle underlies the power of any team. The individual players have clearly defined roles that fit into the whole. Each player is different, yet is committed to the process of maintaining the power of the group.

Beck and Linscott (1991) contend that all types of thinking systems in the spiral need to be integrated into the whole (see figure of the evolutionary spiral in Chapter 4). Each thinking system has something special to offer the whole. The synergy of the whole can only be achieved if each value system is allowed to exist without being threatened and/or denied expression. A healthy spiral respects the differences in value thinking systems.

> 'The Spiral is neither mechanistic nor symmetrical. It has its own internal logic and is rather like a living organism which is held in place by dynamic tension.' (Beck and Linscott, 1991:137)

It is necessary that a dynamic balance exists between the differences in these thinking systems. In this balance, it is inevitable that contradictions and paradoxes need to be integrated. Old traditional thinking only allows one to see one side of the paradox, forcing one to reject or throw away the other side of the paradox – 'either/or' type of thinking. Our mind-sets have trapped us. We have been conditioned to draw distinctions that create watertight compartments, like right/wrong, left/right, capitalism/socialism.

Now is the time for 'both/and' thinking to emerge. The opposing forces actually create the necessary activity and energy for a quantum leap to occur. This is the energy that needs to be directed and utilised. In all negotiations, a co-operative competitiveness needs to prevail, with 'both/and' thinking applied to any dilemma.

The psychology of scarcity has always been evident in Third World countries, while the psychology of abundance operates in technological countries in the First World. Neither of these extremes is healthy. In South Africa, these two psychologies are constantly rubbing shoulders. In time, I believe that this will also become a global issue. A new order needs to emerge.

As the psychology of scarcity and the psychology of abundance interact, tremendous uncertainty and insecurity will surface. Energy will be generated, as these opposing psychologies clash in interaction. I believe that the **psychology of connectedness** will emerge during this interaction (this is not the same as the psychology of equalness). The psychology of connectedness implies that opposing forces need to be integrated. This integration must maintain a dynamic balance between these forces. A more complex order must result. Simply giving away supplies, food and aid is not a long-term solution; this has become evident in the way the First

World have been trying to assist Africa in the past. More complex solutions need to be found in South Africa.

Force will not offer any long-term solution to our problems. The process of integrating diversity can be time consuming and frustrating to some people. There have been significant achievements by all parties as we all try to find the meeting ground. Our history has never allowed us to meet.

The true nature of integration allows differences to coexist in an interdependent manner. Global issues require this type of integration. As we move into the 21st century, old political boundaries will become more and more irrelevant. It is always important to remember that political boundaries are man-made. The pictures of Mother Earth from space show one beautiful globe. One home. There is nowhere else to go.

## MIND IN BUSINESS

Mind in Sport should be able to guide Mind in Business. Systemic and integrative management, that incorporates the principles of ecologic, will be most able to create synergetic working groups that are task focused.

A company is multi-layered with complex, intricate, interdependent connections between sections, departments and individuals. No individual has the same perception of the company. In time, a company develops a culture as individual attitudes and perceptions interact and converge. Patterns of interaction emerge in all companies. These patterns may be political in nature, and therefore, may use vital interpersonal energy that should in fact be directed into task completion.

In order to both survive and grow in the market, a company needs to continually:

1. Focus on itself. This is done in order to maintain and conserve certain cultural values (no change, stability), and also to address obstacles that require change so that growth and development can continue. A company continually has to deal with the opposite forces of change and stability. Resistances to change only

occur if force has been applied. Individuals resent being prescribed to.

2.  Focus on the competitive relationship it has within the market.
    It is important to understand who the opponents are, and how
    the competition between you and the opposition is unfolding.
    Being able to coexist with one's competitor is a more healthy
    focus, than to try and destroy the competition. It becomes more
    important to map out a unique route in the market place for
    your own company.

3.  Focus on wider socio-economic contextual issues. In other
    words, a rapidly changing South Africa will impinge on the
    company. Companies do not operate in a vacuum. As changes
    occur in the wider cultural context, it will be impossible to main-
    tain the same balance and structure in your company. South
    African companies will be forced to address new individual
    aspirations and expectations of those employees from disad-
    vantaged communities. These expectations will need to be
    absorbed by the organisation.

### Business Synergy

In group sports, a team with high synergy achieves success. Each
individual should feel that he is making a valuable contribution to
the whole. A business organisation is like a team. The managing
director can be equated as being the coach. The 'players' may be the
different departments. Alternatively, each department head can be
seen to be the coach with all the employees in the department making up his team.

Each manager will need to examine his own thinking. Team
synergy will emerge through integration of differences. Synergy is
not created by authority or force. Synergy is created through participation in 'reality' linking. The systemic manager will take
everyone's reality into consideration and integrate these into a
committed whole.

A systemic manager has the functioning of the whole team at
heart. He understands the individual differences in the team and
responds differently depending on the nature of the situation. He
keeps the following principles in mind throughout his interaction:

- Everyone is connected to everyone else. Relationships are the links in a team. If one individual is not committed consciously or unconsciously to the team or organisation, then performance in the whole will be lowered.
- The manager is always influencing a situation that he is observing or participating in. His own stresses will be transmitted to the team.
- He should never focus on winning or maximising profits. Peak performance is created if the focus is on the flow of activity in the team. Individuals need to commit themselves to the process. Quality in action becomes the goal. The end product looks after itself.
- The mind always draws distinctions in a situation where interactive tension is evident. As an example, let us examine the distinction of management/union. A dynamic tension will always exist between these elements. This is normal. If a healthy resolution of difficulties is to emerge, then both elements should not be looking at the end result of 'how to win'; but rather involving themselves in healthy interactive participation in decision-making. This will ensure healthy evolutionary change and growth.
- Companies need to think in terms of dilemmas, circles, connections and synergies (Hampden-Turner, 1990). These processes are embedded in Eastern culture, and therefore are accepted in Asian companies. Western organisations tend to be result-orientated, driven by an intense competitiveness of linear thinking.
- Complementary opposites generate the necessary energy for activity. The Yin and Yang flow provide cyclical, harmonious rhythms. There is no maximisation or minimisation of views in any interpersonal situation. Instead, one continually strives to integrate these flows into a harmonious balance. The striving for this balance is continuous. No end point is reached.
- Dynamic balance between opposing forces is the essence of life and healthy evolutionary growth. Quantum leaps occur when the build-up of tension between these forces increases to such a point, that a 'jump' allows for meaningful integrative change. In this sense, change is not forced or prescribed. Imposed prescriptive change will result in unconscious resentments, and reduce the synergy.

It is always important to remember that ideas release vibrations and energy. In a working group, individual differences (ideas) need to be integrated around a common theme. This theme becomes the crystalliser and generator of more energy and power.

It is necessary to build a web of connections (regarding ideas) that link different levels in a company. More specifically, the individual, subgroup and whole team need to be connected in a unifying theme. Refer to the section on linking individual, subgroup and team in Chapter 3.

Companies develop cultures over time. This culture determines individual expectations, as well as dictates patterns of interaction between individual and/or departments within the organisation. A culture of excellence can never be prescribed by higher authority. Instead, a culture of excellence develops within. It develops when each individual in a group commits himself (consciously and unconsciously) to the mission statement and vision of the organisation. This commitment to the culture of the organisation or team is dependent on how each individual perceives:

- how the organisation or group responds to the individual's view regarding a particular issue. How does the group behave towards the individual? What is the group's personality?
- whether he will be able to fulfill his own needs in the group. What can this group offer me?
- whether he is able to contribute meaningfully to the group goal. Am I important to this team?

Some interpersonal patterns of interaction in organisations become destructive. Interpersonal sabotage and infighting use up a great deal of creative energy. In the process, individuals feel unfulfilled and resentful, and an unhealthy functioning culture starts developing. It is important to reflect on how the group or organisation:

- solves problems (focus on any issue and on any organisational level).
- communicates (nature and pattern of information flow). Who is talking to whom, when and about what?

- gives emotional support. Does the culture go beyond work and achievement? Does one really feel cared for, in times of stress?
- defines discipline and quality. A healthy group creates meaningful demands for individuals. A culture of quality is dependent on hard, dedicated effort at work.

These are the most important elements in generating a synergetic organisation, that continually strives for quality in action.

## Redefining Profits

At present, South Africa finds itself economically stretched to breaking point. The 'fat' years are over. While our currency continues to shrink on the international market, businesses also have to contend with the ever changing political situation. Further, more and more convergence and mixing of First and Third world pressures are occurring within organisations.

The existing conditions are creating internal stress on organisations. For some, the future may appear bleak. As businesses move into the 21st century, the psychology of success may have to take on a different meaning.

Profitability will need to be redefined. The flow of profits will not be in accordance with the assumption that more is possible each day. Refer back to Figure 2 in Chapter 3 on the assumption that sporting performance gets better and better in exponential fashion. Instead, executives will need to think more in terms of upward and downward flow regarding financial profits.

Successful companies will have the ability to survive in the marketplace during the downward flows. They will have the ability to remain focused on providing a quality of service and/or product that goes beyond money.

The focus of any company striving for success will be on the network of relationships existing within the company, and the relationships that exist between company and clients. 'Profitability' (defined in terms of meaningful contact to ensure coexistence) in relationships will become extremely important. Coexistence implies co-dependence.

Exploiting a client in whatever way may lead to possible extinction. A company needs a client in order to survive. In fact, the existence of a company is defined in terms of what the company can offer a client. It is in the client relationship that 'profits' are made.

Focusing on the needs of the client will ensure the best possible chance of success. A company will be perceived as being a 'winner' only if a client feels that his/their needs have been satisfied.

A culture of excellence in a company is achieved if each individual employee is committed to achieving his/her individual goal. In the past, companies may have exploited their employees in some way in order to maximise financial profits. This may have stirred up emotional resentments. If exploitation continues, confrontations with unions may result. An escalation of aggression between management and union will use a great deal of company energy and reduce the power and synergy of the company. There will be no winners if this process continues.

The company must be able to balance actual financial profits with employee benefits. A company may not show remarkable financial end-of-year profits, yet may be interpersonally successful and resilient. During economic hardship and stress, employees who are connected to the whole, will commit themselves fully to the company to ensure continuation of existence.

When the going gets tough, the possibility of fragmentation of a group increases. It is the vital links that exist between people that are most fragile in any team or company. A winning team is a happy team. A happy team has developed a togetherness that ensures that each individual is acknowledged for the part that he plays in making the whole so powerful. The company's success depends upon the feeling that the journey is worthwhile and meaningful, no matter how tough or painful.

Achieving oneness and peak performance in an organisation reflects the essence of true profitability.

Finally, a company cannot be separated from the environment. Companies will be forced to become more aware of ecological factors. Any decision that is made by the company will feed back into the company in some way, on some level. A circular connectedness exists. Decisions that exploit or maximise a given situation in order to make substantial short-term profit, may prove to be unwise in the long term. The fabric of life consists of a connected web of links. In maintaining and nurturing these links, the fabric of the organisation will continue to exist and evolve in the market.

### Executive Stress

Executive stress is the result of being unbalanced in some way on some level. In discussion with managers regarding stress at work, I became aware that they are searching for techniques to relieve the stress, without wanting to restructure or change their own lifestyles or work contexts. There is a belief that they have to learn to cope better.

I believe that stress reactions are important messages that need to be listened to. They are trying to tell you something about:

- yourself and the way that you are trying to deal with things;
- others you are involved with;
- the situation that you find yourself in.

Stress over time starts manifesting itself in the body and in behaviour. Headaches, heart palpitations, ulcers, insomnia, excessive alcohol consumption, irregular eating, irritability, loss of libido, ill-health over time, are some of the signs of being under excessive stress. One must take these signals very seriously. Burnout and physical or mental breakdown results if a person does not heed and respond appropriately to these signals.

People generate stress. This is important to remember. Stress is primarily generated by 'going against the grain' in situations. As one responds in these situations, one can feel an invisible wall or something pulling one back. This drains energy. It tires one.

One's mind (ideas and thoughts) directs action. If you believe that making five thousand rand a day is important and reflects success, then you will push into situations and try and force interactional processes in order to achieve this success.

Forcing the pace in processes generates resistance. Nature has certain time periods for processes. Pregnancy, for example, takes nine months. If you try and speed the process and reduce the time (I am sure that our quantitative scientists would try and develop ways of doing this), then you will increase the chances of deformity in the child. A common cold or flu takes a certain time period in each individual to work itself out of the system.

Completing a job also has a time process to it. Information flow also has a time process. In today's competitive business world, everything has a deadline that seems to be 'yesterday'. Everybody is activated, everybody rushing. Managers generate a great deal of stress, due to unrealistic expectations regarding time periods for completion of quality tasks.

While I do agree that there may be certain times when one has to push ahead relentlessly to complete projects, I tend to question the reasons of continual pressure and rushing in work contexts. There is something wrong if this becomes a norm. Work, like sport, should flow effortlessly in most situations. During my military service, there was a saying: 'Hurry up and wait'. In the work context, become aware of who and what is chasing you. Do not use vital, creative energy in chasing after your own tail, only for the sake of saying that you are doing something.

In some organisations (especially government bureaucracies), individuals often 'play' busy. It seems that free time in company time is taboo. So instead of generating a creative focus for possible future projects in the available free time, individuals waste precious reflective time to show 'somebody' (I always wonder who this somebody really is – maybe big Daddy?) that they are 'working'. This happens throughout the whole organisation, on all managerial levels.

If you are having to rush and operate under stress constantly, then a re-evaluation of your lifestyle and the demands that your work environment are placing on you, needs to be carefully considered. Any interpersonal activity must always consider the complexity or conditions that are prevailing in a situation. In order to do this, it is necessary to examine your own beliefs and expectations.

The first question that I would want you to consider is: What is success?

This is an extremely important question, since your answer will create certain expectations regarding the way you interact in your home and work situations. Your answer will also direct your energy flow while you are interacting with others.

Achieving success (still needs to be defined) is rewarding. However, be careful of not linking your self-worth to achievement of possessions. Some people can only feel happy if they can see what they have achieved. This view, is in line with the rules of mechologic (refer to Chapter 4), and needs to be confronted.

Success has all too often been very narrowly defined. It has invariably only been linked to finance and/or possessions. I believe that this definition needs to be broadened. Success should include the ability to maintain a balance in all situations; a balance regarding work and home; between contrasting views; in terms of diet; a balance between relaxation and hard work.

Nature has provided very ordinary methods to relieve stress: sleep, relaxation and exercise. Simple methods, but very effective.

One always hears the typical response to the suggestion of a change in the lifestyle of a stressed person: 'But I have no time. I have so much to do'. Remember that stress reactions are nature's message that something is wrong and that you need to address your lifestyle. We all fall into patterns of interaction that are difficult to break or change. The problem with stress reactions, however, is that either you can consciously decide to introduce more balance in your living, or nature will decide for you in terms of a crisis (breakdown on some level). Those are the simple alternatives. Stress will not disappear on its own. You are the generator of your stress.

We are not machines. Trying to maximise financial success at the expense of other activities is dangerous. You will suddenly find yourself on the roller-coaster and not be able to get off. A spiralling runaway!

The second question I would want you to consider is: How can I relinquish control and responsibility in work situations, without concern about sacrificing quality?

The answer to this question is to be found in how you create synergy and commitment in your company. I have already discussed this in detail. Autocratic decision making heightens stress levels in the long run. This style may 'work' in the short term, but will be unable to generate its own energy over time. It will struggle to sustain itself. It will always require the force and motivation of an external higher power to get individuals to work.

The result of this will be that all of the responsibility and control will be pushed onto the shoulders of the autocratic manager. This burden is very heavy to carry alone.

The section on coaching styles (Chapter 4) is relevant here. I believe that coaches, like managers, take on too much responsibility in getting things to work in teams. The concepts of 'shared responsibility' and 'awareness and process coaching' need to apply in work contexts. In this way, the company's total stress is spread across the whole organisation in a fair way.

The third question that I want to ask you is: What other interests do you have, besides work?

I was consulted by an executive (in his mid-thirties) who was suffering from stress and depression. He had been very successful in his work, yet somehow felt 'empty'. He had thrown all his energies, time and effort into work. In the process, he had lost his own identity. He could only define himself in terms of his work. There was nothing else to him, except work. He was unable to find any other sphere of activity where he could generate meaningful feedback about himself.

The fourth and last question that I would want you to consider is: What is my role in the family (if married) or, what is the nature of my more intimate relationships?

Close relationships are always first to suffer when a person is under stress. Trying to interact in a family, feeling exhausted, with little or no energy, inadvertently creates more potential for stress. Family members need to have some part of you. Children want a father, wives want a husband, friend and lover. Therefore, family members will unconsciously try and activate and involve you by confronting you with mundane family issues. In this way, the family will start feeding into the stress cycle, when they experience you as being exhausted and tired, with nothing to give.

A family will only be a place to release stress, if you do not always hide and withdraw. It will become necessary to involve yourself in some family activities in order to develop the relationships in the family team. If you do not resent this involvement, it can become an extremely fulfilling part of life. Nurturing the growth and development of one's children is exciting. Becoming playful with one's children can release built -up tension and generate new creativity within. The balance between work and home needs to be maintained.

A South African manager has to deal with far more uncertainty, complexity and chaos in the business environment than any of his 'brothers' in the technologically advanced First World countries. This heightens stress. The changing face of the new South Africa will add further pressure.

I believe that executives do not have enough time for reflective thinking (thinking about your thinking), visualisation or meditation. These are processes that regenerate energy, require a move inwards, and release stress and tension.

It is so important that you look after yourself (mind and body). This is your biggest responsibility. There are lots of people who depend on your wellbeing.

## CHAPTER 7

# Where to from here?

In formulating my ideas regarding mind in sport, I recognise that I have attempted to freeze-frame the complex activity that occurs between mind and body during action. For a writer, this is a near impossible task. Nevertheless, the book has had as its focus, the nature of mind during sporting action (and the build-up to that action).

I believe that these ideas regarding the mind in activity, go beyond sport. Life is activity. The only thing that changes in life is the context. The fundamental concepts of energy flow and connectedness remain. Relationships are the vital links in the fabric of life. This is also true for sport.

Allowing time for quiet reflective thinking is an important part of a sportsman's mental preparation. This type of thinking should ensure detachment from the situation that one is involved in. Creating a focused mind-set in this time allows one the opportunity to utilise the mind's energy in order to achieve what you have set out to accomplish. Visualisation, meditation, or 'detached reflection' are mental processes that create a mind-set to ensure achievement of goals.

A culture of excellence can best be achieved if an athlete is able to focus and flow during activity. This allows the mind to direct action (focus), yet allowing the body to move freely and spontaneously (flow). In the flow period, a sportsman operates in the 'no mind' state. Physical energy is released without thinking. In the process, a mind-body integration occurs and a powerful oneness is achieved.

The striving for quality in action (in whatever is done) is the hallmark of a champion. Striving for excellence is at the core of the psychology of winning. Each moment presented in time should be fully utilised. 'Become the moment' is a statement that best illustrates the moulding of mind and body into the situation.

The concept of dynamic balance is at the core of peak performance. Being able to integrate the forces or conditions that are operating in a given situation creates synergetic power. With reference to groups, integrating different perspectives (or energy forces) is vital, if a quantum leap is to be achieved during performance.

An important component in achieving success is the ability to maintain the dynamic balance between arousal and relaxed performance. An inner awareness, helps the athlete to keep in touch with his body during activity.

The nature of the relationship between coach and player determines the type of energy flow that will emerge both off and on the field. The new paradigm of ecosystemic principles provides the framework of how one should think about thinking. Any interactive process between people is circular and connective. Any thought (conscious or unconscious) will determine the direction and nature of energy flow of the individual, as well as influence the strength of the synergetic wholeness of a team.

As South African sport continues to develop and evolve in international competition, the issues confronting sporting administrators need to be handled with creativity and not with force. We find ourselves in a time of history where so much is happening so quickly. While this is exciting and challenging, it does require managing and directing complex interpersonal and group processes with care and support. It is important to be pro-active, but not autocratic. There is a big difference between these styles of interaction.

As we continue to evolve and move on in time, our children become our most precious commodity. The fundamental force in nature is to ensure that a species can cope with the conditions of existence that are prevailing at a given time in history. Each generation becomes better equipped mentally and physically to deal with the complexities in situations that occur in the environment.

Man's arrogance and interference in trying to maximise or minimise situations for his own selfish ends, however, has lead him to a dead end. A major shift in thinking is now required: a quantum leap in thinking. This can best be achieved in the minds of our children. In talking to young children, I have become aware that they intuitively understand 'the nature of things'.

Recently, I was witness to a most interesting family discussion. The context of the discussion is that famous conversation pit; the dinner table. This is an ordinary middle class family consisting of Dad, Mom, Wayne (11 years) and Gareth (9 years).

Gareth: Did you send me to club soccer to have fun or to be serious? (the question being directed to Mom)

Mom: Uhm.... (no immediate answer – obviously taken aback by this major dilemma that is facing Gareth)

Wayne: (quickly jumping into the silence) I hate it when you are always told what to do when you are playing. Everybody is just shouting at you, telling you how to play.

Gareth: Yes, and all you want to do is to have some fun.

Wayne : Gareth, but you can't always just have fun.

Dad : When he is not having fun, what should he then be doing, Wayne?

Gareth: Yes, Wayne..what should I then be doing? (becoming intense)

Mom : Gareth, why did you ask me that question? (has now regained her composure)

Gareth: Mom, the coach at soccer said that we were all messing around during the match....and that we must decide whether we want to take it seriously or .. JUST HAVE FUN. (now mimicking the tone and body language of the coach)

Wayne : (trying to act mature) Yes Gareth, you small guys are always messing around. During our matches, we always try our best.

Mom : Quiet, Wayne. (trying to maintain contact with Gareth)

Gareth: Yes Wayne, shut up! (tension building between Wayne and Gareth)

Mom : Gareth, do you think that you were messing around in the match? (This question creates an uneasiness in Gareth)

Dad :      I would like to get back to the question of what you will
           be doing with yourself if you don't have fun?

Wayne:    (Immediate response) Trying your best, of course.

Gareth:   But, Dad, we were really trying our best in the match.

Mom :     Maybe the coach did not think that you were trying your
          best.

Wayne :   Yes, Gareth maybe he knows that the team did not try
          their best. (confidently stating a certain truth)

Gareth:   (A bit confused) But, how would he know if we are trying
          our best? (This is a complex question and could now real-
          ly lead this discussion into the labyrinth of life)

Mom :     Gareth, a coach tries to teach you how to play properly.
          He guides you, and helps you...

Wayne :   (interrupting Mom) And shouts at you.

Gareth:   I get sad when people shout at me.

Mom :     I know that, Gareth. Sometimes pressure makes people
          shout.
          (A thoughtful silence prevails)

Gareth:   What is pressure?
          (More silence)

Mom :     I've been wondering whether it isn't possible to join fun
          and 'trying hard' together.

Dad :     The trick is to have serious fun while trying your best.
          (Mom, Wayne and Gareth look at Dad as if he is a smart
          Alec)

Mom :     Gareth, it is always important that you enjoy your sport.
          You can always feel this in your heart. While playing,
          remember also to try hard. You should also feel this in
          your heart. Only you will know. And this is the only
          thing that matters.

All significant adults (teachers, coaches, parents) need to become aware of the realities that they are creating for children. It is important to journey with a child as he or she grapples with the complexities in a situation. There are no easy answers.

As the complexity in our thinking continues to evolve over time, I have no doubt that new insights regarding performance will emerge. This is the nature of things. Ideas often become outdated once they are formulated. This will also apply to this book.

However, for me, this book has a deeper meaning. It reflects some elements of my own journey over a two-year period.

The book completed full circle two days after Natal won the 1992 Currie Cup rugby final, when it was accepted for publication. Its conception occurred when I first became involved with Natal in their historic 1990 Currie Cup victory.

New challenges lie ahead.

# Appendix

## Jimmy Cook

Jimmy Cook has a remarkable cricket record. Despite his shock omission from the World Cup cricket team, Jimmy remained dignified and quiet. He is highly respected in world cricket. In the years of our cricket isolation, Jimmy was the only South African player to play in every one-day and five-day international test matches, starting with the rebel English team led by Graham Gooch in 1982, and culminating in being selected as captain against the rebel English team led by Mike Gatting in 1989. His three seasons playing county cricket for Somerset (1989, 1990, 1991) were phenomenally successful, with him scoring over 2 000 first class runs in each of the seasons. He topped the English County batting averages in the 1989 and 1991 seasons. Besides cricket, Jimmy also played First Division professional soccer for Wits University for nine years. He was considered to be an above-average central defender and sweeper. He retired from football at the age of 31, having pursued both top class cricket and soccer for nine years. The intense demands of both sports eventually resulted in his retirement from soccer.

## Bruce Fordyce

Bruce Fordyce is an athletic genius. He has won the Comrades Marathon (Durban – Pietermaritzburg: 89 Kilometres) on nine occasions. His first win was in 1981, and he remained unbeaten till 1991. Bruce also holds both the up and down records. Bruce is a true professional and has become a running legend. He has developed a wealth of inner knowledge through his own learning and experiences while competing. He conducts workshops for athletes intending to run Comrades, and writes a weekly newspaper column where he discusses issues pertinent to the ordinary runner. On the international circuit, he has competed in the London to Brighton Marathon on three occasions (1981, 1982, 1983), winning them all. He holds the record of 5hrs 12min 32sec set in 1983 for the 53mile 1082yd distance. In 1987 he won the Arctic Marathon (again setting the record of 6hr 34min 37sec for the 84Km distance). He again competed in this ultra-marathon in July, 1992, and won the race in record time of 6hr 21min (12 minutes better than his previous record). In 1989 Bruce did not run the Comrades. Instead, he competed in an internationally sponsored 100 Km challenge race in Stellenbosch. He finished first in a field of the world's top best ultra-marathon runners.

### Brian Mitchell

Brian Mitchell is South Africa's undefeated World Junior Lightweight boxing champion. He retired in January 1992, with both the World Boxing Association (WBA) and the International Boxing Federation (IBF) titles. He successfully defended his WBA championship crown on 12 occasions, after winning the world title against Alfredo Layne on the 27th September 1986. Brian has an impressive professional fighting record: 47 fights, 43 wins (of which 20 were KO's), three draws, with one loss. Brian has achieved a number of awards. He received the State President Sportsman of the Year award for six successive years, from 1986 to 1991. Most recently, Brian was named the South African Sportsman of the decade. Brian's success in the ring has been the result of dedicated commitment and discipline. Despite all his achievements, there is a humbleness and sincerity about him. Brian is a deep thinking person. He stated that his decision to retire required as much mental preparation and toughness as any of his world title fights.

### *Jonty Rhodes*

Jonty Rhodes is a double international sportsman in cricket and hockey. He was picked for the South African hockey squad for an internal test match series in 1991. To date, he has not officially represented South Africa in a hockey test match. Having worked with the national side in their mental preparation, I have no doubt that Jonty has the ability to officially represent his country on the hockey field. Being young and vibrant, Jonty has a wonderful future ahead of him. He proved to be a tremendous success at the World Cup cricket tournament in Australia, and has added a new dimension to cricket with his dynamic approach to fielding. His sensational run out of the Pakistani batsman Inzamam when he dived at the stumps seems to be imprinted in every youngster's mind. Jonty told me that most of his fanmail focuses on how he is able to dive so well. Just one remarkable sporting incident has generated tremendous interest in the art of fielding.

# Bibliography

Auwerswald, D (1990): *Comparing Paradigms: Mechologic and ecologic*. A workshop presented at the University of South Africa, Pretoria.

Bateson, G (1979): *Mind and Nature*. Toronto: Bantam.

Baynes, C and Boardman, WS (1984): *The Pocket I Ching*. London: Arkana.

Beck, D and Linscott, G (1991): *The Crucible: Forging South Africa's future*. Honeydew: New Paradigm Press.

Benson, H (1975): *The Relaxation Response*. New York: William Morrow & Company.

Brandon, D (1976): *Zen in the Art of Helping*. London: Arkana.

Capra, F (1982): *The Turning Point: Science, society and the rising culture*. London: Flamingo.

Capra, F (1988): *Uncommon Wisdom*. London: Flamingo.

Cleary, T (1986): *The Taoist I Ching*. Boston: Shambhala.

Csikszentmihalyi, M (1991): Flow: The psychology of optimal experience. An article published in *The Star*, 10 December 1991.

De Shazer, S (1985): *Keys to Solution in Brief Therapy*. New York: Norton.

Dreher, D (1990): *The Tao of Peace: A modern guide to the ancient way of peace and harmony*. London: Mandala.

Galante, L (1981): *Tai Chi: The supreme ultimate*. York Beach: Weisner.

Gallwey, TW (1976): *The Inner Game of Tennis*. London: Pan Books.

Gallwey, TW (1986): *The Inner Game of Golf*. London: Pan Books.

Garfield, CA (1985): *Peak Performance: Mental training techniques of the world's greatest athletes*. Los Angeles: Warner Books.

Gawain, S (1982): *Creative Visualization*. Toronto: Bantam.

Gendlin, E (1981): *Focusing*. New York: Bantam.

Hampden-Turner, C (1990): *Charting the Corporate Mind: From dilemma to strategy*. Oxford: Blackwell.

Harding, DE (1986): *On Having No Head: Zen and the re-discovery of the obvious*. London: Arkana.

Hyams, J (1982): *Zen in the Martial Arts*. New York: Bantam.

Jennings, KE (1991): *The Rhythm of Sport*. Paper presented at the Second International Conference on Sport and Recreation: A bridge to the future. Rand Afrikaans University, Johanesburg.

Jennings, KE (1991): *Music – A Relaxer and Arouser: Transcending obstacles*. Workshop presented at the Annual Congress of the Psychological Association of South Africa, University of Pretoria.

Jennings, KE (1992): What excites you about the sport you play? *Junior Sports Magazine*, May 1992. (Unpublished).

Jennings, KE (1992): *Creating Images: A story of differences*. Workshop presented at the Biennial International Conference of the South African Institute of Marital and Family Therapy, held in Durban.

Kadowaki, J (1989): *Zen and the Bible: A priest's experience*. London: Arkana.

Keeney, B (1983): *Aesthetics of Change*. New York: Guilford Press.

Kushner, K (1988): *One Arrow, One Life: Zen, archery, and daily life*. London: Arkana.

Lash, J (1989): *The Tai Chi Journey*. Shaftsbury: Element.

Page, M (1989): *The Tao of Power: An eastern way to a greener world*. London: Merlin Press.

Pirsig, R (1974): *Zen and the Art of Motorcycle Maintenance*. London: Corgi.

Robbins, A (1986): *Unlimited Power: The new science of personal achievement*. London: Simon & Schuster.

Rogers, C (1967): *A Therapist's View of Psychotherapy: On becoming a person*. London: Constable & Company.

Van der Wetering, J (1987): *The Empty Mirror: Experiences in a Japanese zen monastery*. London: Arkana.

Watzlawick, P, Beavin, JH and Jackson, DD (1967): *Pragmatics of Human Communication*. New York: W W Norton.

Watzlawick, P, Weakland, JH and Fisch, R (1974): *Change: Principles of problem formation and problem resolution*. New York: W W Norton.

West, KL, Calder, S and Bressan, ES (1992): *The effects of visual skills training and sports-specific vision coaching on the skill performance of elite-level field hockey players*. University of Stellenbosch. Unpublished manuscript.

Zdenek, M (1985): *The Right-Brain Experience*. London: Corgi.

# *Index*

## A

acceptance   13, 20, 21, 23, 99
achievement   1, 4, 15, 21, 29, 50, 51, 53, 56, 96, 134, 150, 181, 197, 201
activity   26, 47, 48, 51, 63, 80, 88, 91, 92, 95, 99, 125, 164, 192, 200, 205
   natural breaks   25, 47, 62, 66-67
   non-action   25, 89
   simple   4, 8, 15, 148
administrators   33, 65, 114-115, 117, 118, 181, 187, 206
advertising   151, 180
anxious   94
arousal   93, 95, 137, 141, 142, 154, 162, 164
athletics   121, 182
awareness   14, 15, 21, 27, 34-39, 41, 53, 61, 103, 117, 126-127, 144,
   146, 153, 175, 206

## B

balance   25, 26, 34, 44, 48-54, 88, 89, 95, 101, 117, 180, 188, 195, 199,
   201, 203
   delicate   3, 122
   dynamic   3, 30, 34, 36, 37, 39, 43, 56, 58, 60, 137, 139, 165, 175,
      191-193, 206
   in movement   53
   in thinking   5
   mind–body   2, 14, 24, 25, 27, 37, 38, 48, 60, 147, 161
   of forces   2, 36, 48, 191
body
   grooving   14-16, 37, 53, 95, 120
   learning   16
   language   9, 52, 81, 96, 117
   message   23, 24, 35, 42, 126
   sensation   24, 27, 36, 39, 42, 127, 153, 166